W9-AAU-898

PROTOCOLS REFUTED
DESTROYING THE FRAUD

TimeWorthy Books
P. O. Box 30000
Phoenix, AZ 85046-0009

ISBN: 0-935199-02-0

All Scripture references are taken from the New King James Version of the Bible, unless otherwise noted.

Printed in the United States of America.

INTRODUCTION

With every fiber of my being, I will refute every word of the "*Protocols of the Learned Elders of Zion.*"

This is not just some "fantasy" book that some people took to heart, and then did some evil. This book has done more harm than any other book, when it comes to the Jewish race.

MILLIONS of Jews have been murdered because of this literary fraud.

When I visit Israel, I personally know many families who have suffered greatly because of the perils of this book.

PROTOCOLS REFUTED is something that I wish would become a permanent solution. In spite of governments denigrating this book, and proving that this book is a fraud, yet millions of people still cling to this travesty and believe that every word in it is true.

Please follow my typed commentary below the copy of each page of the original book and my handwritten notes in red. Quite frankly, these notes were hard to write; as I realized that every word of the original *Protocols* is a ghastly fake.

I trust that your heart is in much prayer for the Jewish people as you read this book. They have suffered so brutally as a direct consequence of anti-Semitics clinging to the writings in Protocols.

My hope is that you will urge others to help destroy this wicked fraud.

As Islamic Shariah Law overtakes the earth, it is my anticipation that you and your friends will stand up for what is right; to stand up against ANY form of anti-Semitism. We must never permit the Enemy to win.

And, believe me, just as the Bible proclaims, we are against "powers and principalities!" Are you ready for the fight? I am!

Thank you for "digesting" this book and standing with me in support of Israel!

—Mike Evans

The Jewish Peril

PROTOCOLS

OF THE

Learned Elders of Zion.

SECOND EDITION.

Published by "THE BRITONS," 62 Oxford Street London, W.

1920.

Price, 3/- Net.

S.

The Jew-Bolshevic Emblem, surrounded by the Symbolic Serpent. See *Protocol III.*, p. 10.

PREFATORY NOTE TO THE SECOND EDITION.

Messrs. Eyre & Spottiswoode having disposed of their rights in this work to the present publishers, it has not been thought necessary to make any alteration in the text; but, as the numbering of the Protocols is not indicated, a Note has been appended to the volume which will enable readers to add the numbers in their proper places in the margins.

On May 8th, 1920, *The Times* published an article on this work which it called "A Disturbing Pamphlet: a Call for Enquiry." Since then, in a series of articles commencing July 12, the *Morning Post* has published a very exhaustive "enquiry," under the title of "The World Unrest." The Protocols the writer very fitly names "THE BOLSHEVIST BIBLE." He proves by a mass of cumulative historic evidence that the Protocols are Jewish, and that a secret organisation of Jews is at the base of the world's unrest. The *Times* writer says that no one can fail to recognise Soviet Russia in the Protocols, and it asks, "Whence comes the uncanny note of prophecy, prophecy in part fulfilled, in parts far gone in the way of fulfilment? Have we been struggling these tragic years to blow up and extirpate the secret organisation of German world dominion only to find beneath it *another more dangerous* because *more secret*? Have we, by straining every fibre of our national body, escaped a 'Pax Germanica' only to fall into a 'PAX JUDÆICA'?" The answer, as supplied by the *Morning Post's* articles, and by the facts of the present day—strikes, revolutions, high prices, shortage, speculation, and unrest everywhere—is that *this is exactly what we have fallen into*—a JEWISH "PEACE!"

We commend this "disturbing pamphlet" to the most serious consideration of all true Britons. The Kaiser was not the real enemy, egregious sinner though he was. The Learned Elders of Zion were behind him, and it is they who have now to be squarely met.

PREFACE.

AT a moment when the whole of Western Europe is enlarging upon the benefits of constitutional governments and discussing on the one hand the merits and on the other the sins of Maximalism (Bolshevism), I think that I may with advantage put before the English-speaking public, the translation of a book published at Tsarskoye Sielo, in Russia, in the year 1905.

A copy of the original may be seen at the British Museum Library, under No. 3926 d 17, stamped British Museum, 10th August, 1906. How many more copies of the book may be seen in the world, I can hardly say, as, shortly after its appearance in 1905, most copies seem to have been bought up simultaneously and apparently with a purpose. On this point I would only warn my readers that they must not take a copy of this translation to Russia, as anybody in whose possession it is found by the Bolsheviki is immediately shot, as being the bearer of "reactionary propaganda."

The book was presented to the Russian public by Professor Sergyei Nilus.

It contains:—

(i) An introduction to the main text, written by Sergyei Nilus in 1905.

(ii) Notes on lectures delivered to Jewish students in Paris in the year 1901.

(iii) A portion of an cpilogue written by the same Sergyci Nilus. I have not considered it necessary to reproduce the whole of the epilogue,

This book was first published with the help of the Russian secret police, siding with those against the Bolsheviks in their Russian Revolution!

as portions of it would be of no interest to the British public, and do not bear upon the question before me, namely, that of the Jewish Peril.

I would ask my readers to bear in mind that the lectures above referred to were delivered in 1901, and that Nilus's Introduction and Epilogue were written in 1905.

It is impossible to read any of the parts of this volume to-day without being struck by the strong prophetic note which runs through them all, not only as regards the once Holy Russia, but also as regards certain sinister developments, which may be observed at the present moment throughout the whole world.

Gentiles—Beware!

London,
2nd December, 1919.

This is an outright lie! This book was totally made up, and should have been treated as "fiction!"

This book was meant to scare the Christians by making up a supposed secret Jewish plot to rule the world.

INTRODUCTION.

A MANUSCRIPT has been handed to me by a personal friend, now deceased, which with extraordinary precision and clearness describes the plan and development of a sinister world-wide conspiracy, having for its object that of bringing the unregenerate World to its inevitable dismemberment.

This document came into my possession some four years ago (1901), with the positive assurance that it is a true copy in translation, of original documents stolen by a woman from one of the most influential and most highly initiated leaders of Freemasonry.* The theft was accomplished at the close of a secret meeting of the "initiated" in France, that nest of "Jewish masonic conspiracy."

To those who would see and hear, I venture to reveal this manuscript under the title of "The Protocols of the Elders of Zion." On first scanning through these minutes, they might convey the impression of being what we usually call truisms, and appear to be more or less ordinary truths, though expressed with a pungency and a hatred which does not usually accompany ordinary truths. There seethes between the lines that arrogant and deep-rooted racial and religious hatred, which has been so long successfully concealed, and it bubbles over and flows, as it were, from an overfilled vessel of rage and revenge, fully conscious that its triumphant end is near.

We cannot omit to remark that its title does not altogether correspond to its contents. These are not exactly minutes of meetings, but a report made by some

* Orient Freemasonry.

This is a very bold statement, totally untrue, but it tries to implicate the Jews as "dismembering" the world! Rubbish!

The Jews were lumped together with the Freemasons in this vile worldwide plot! This way you also know this is a false writing.

Just the use of repugnant words, like "seethes" lets you know right away that "God's Chosen People" did NOT write this atrocity!

powerful person, divided into sections not always in a logical sequence. They convey the impression of being the part of something threatening and more important, the beginning of which is missing. The aforementioned origin of this document speaks for itself.

By the prophecies of the Holy Fathers, Anti-Christ's doings must always be a parody on Christ's life, and must have likewise their Judas. But, of course, from an earthly point of view, its Judas will not achieve his ends; thus, although of brief duration, a complete victory of the "world ruler" is assured. This reference to W. Soloviev's words is not intended to be used as a proof of their scientific authority. From an eschatological point of view, science is out of place, the important part is fate. Soloviev gives us the canvas, the embroidery will be worked by the proposed manuscript.

We might be justly reproached with the apocryphal nature of this document; but were it possible to prove this world-wide conspiracy by means of letters or by declarations of witnesses, and if its leaders could be unmasked holding its sanguinary threads, the "mysteries of iniquity," would by this very fact, be violated. To prove itself, it has to remain unmolested till the day of its incarnation in the "son of perdition."

In the present complications of criminal proceedings we cannot look for direct proofs, but we have to be satisfied with circumstantial evidence, and with such the mind of every indignant Christian observer is filled.

That which is written in this work ought to suffice for those "who have ears to hear" as being obvious and is offered them with the intention of urging them to protect themselves while there is yet time, and to be on their guard. Our conscience will be satisfied if by the grace of

There is no proof that the Jews wrote this. The demons who produced this false work even admit there is no written proof!

God we attain this most important aim of warning the Gentile world without exciting in its heart wrath against the blinded people of Israel. We trust that the Gentiles will not entertain feelings of hatred against the erroneously believing mass of Israel in its innocence of the Satanic sin of its leaders—the Scribes and Pharisees—who have already once proved themselves to be the destruction of Israel. Turning aside the wrath of God, there remains but one way—union of all Christians in Our Lord Jesus Christ and total extermination—repentance for ourselves and for others.

But is this possible in the present unregenerate condition of the world? It is impossible for the world, but still possible for believing Russia. The present political conditions of Western European states and of their affiliated countries in other continents were prophesied by the Prince of Apostles. Mankind in its aspiration to perfect its terrestrial life and in its search of a better realisation of the idea of power, which could secure everybody's well-being, and in its quest of a reign of universal satiety, which has become the highest ideal of human life, has changed the direction of its ideals by pronouncing the Christian faith as entirely discredited and not having justified the hopes bestowed on it. Overthrowing former idols, creating new ones, and raising new gods on to pedestals, the world erects for them temples, one more luxurious and more magnificent than the other, and again deposes and destroys them. Mankind has lost the very conception of the power granted by God to kings anointed, and is approaching the conditions of anarchy. Soon the swivel of the republican and constitutional scales will be worn through. The scales will collapse, and in their fall will carry away all the governments to the very abyss of raging anarchy.

The "author" of this fabricated document, says that the Jews are the "blinded" people. To the contrary, the Jews are enlightened!

The Jewish people would never discredit the Christian faith.

This is meant to bolster the importance of the Russians!

The world's last rampart and last refuge from the coming storm is Russia. Her true faith is still alive, and the anointed Emperor still stands as her sure protector.

All the efforts of destruction on the part of the sinister and evident servants of the * Anti-Christ, his conscious and unconscious workers, are concentrated on Russia. The reasons are understood, the objects are known, they must be known to believing and faithful Russia. The more threatening the coming historical moment is, the more frightening the approaching events concealed in the dense clouds are, the more courageously and with greater determination the brave and intrepid hearts of the Russians must beat. Bravely ought they to join hands round the sacred banner of their Church and round the throne of their Emperor. So long as the soul lives, so long also the flaming heart beats in the bosom, there is no room for the deathly spectre of despair; but it is for us, and for our fidelity, to gain the Almighty's mercy and to delay the hour of Russia's fall (1905).

* Can you imagine the audacity of this writer calling the Jews "servants of the Anti-Christ?!"

This fictitious literary "work" meant to frighten the Russians about the false, sinister plot by the Jews to overtake the entire world!

PROTOCOLS OF THE ELDERS OF ZION.

WE will be plainspoken and discuss the significance of each reflection, and by comparisons and deductions we will produce full explanations. By this means I will expose the conception of our policy and that of the Goys (*i.e.*, Jewish definition of all Gentiles). It must be noted that people with corrupt instincts are more numerous than those of noble instinct. Therefore in governing the world the best results are obtained by means of violence and intimidation, and not by academic discussions. Every man aims at power; everyone would like to become a dictator if he only could do so, and rare indeed are the men who would not be disposed to sacrifice the welfare of others in order to attain their own personal aims.

What restrained the wild beasts of prey which we call men? What has ruled them up to now? In the first stages of social life they submitted to brute and blind force, then to law, which in reality is the same force, only masked. From this I am led to deduct that by the law of nature, right lies in might. Political freedom is not a fact, but an idea. This idea one must know how to apply when it is necessary, in order to use the same as a bait to attract the power of the populace to one's party, if such party has decided to usurp the power of a rival. The problem is simplified if the said rival becomes infected with ideas of freedom, so-called liberalism, and for the sake of this idea yields some of his power.

Protocol Number 1 of 24 is the "Basic Doctrine" of this fraudulent book.

The Bible says that we are ALL born into sin.

God's Word tells us that man is created in the image of God. Humankind is special; not "wild beasts of prey!"

Millions of my Jewish brothers and sisters have already given their very lives because of this one horrific book. But even more unsettling is that this book, *"Protocols of the Learned Elders of Zion"* is a complete and absolute fraud.

Other than the Bible, this one book has been printed more than any other book in the 1900's. The Jewish people desperately cringe and know its contents all too well. However, most Christians and Gentiles have never even heard of it. How dreadful! This atrocious publication has caused more suffering of the Jewish people in the last century than any other single manuscript. That's why I appeal to you that people should know about its content and ghastly results.

As I have travelled around the world, more important than politics or religion—people are controlled by money and their economy! But Shariah Law is spreading like wildfire across the globe! <u>BEWARE!</u>

In this the triumph of our idea will become apparent. The relinquished reins of government by the law of life are immediately seized by a new hand, because the blind strength of the populace cannot exist for a single day without a leader, and the new government only fills the place of the old, which has been weakened by its liberalism.

Nowadays the power of gold has superseded liberal rulers. There was a time when religion ruled. The idea of freedom is not realisable, because no one knows how to use it with discretion.

It suffices to give the populace self-government for a short period for this populace to become a disorganised rabble. From that very moment dissensions start which soon develop into social battles; the States are set in flames and their total significance vanishes. Whether the state is exhausted by its own internal convulsions, or whether civil wars hand it over to an external foe, it can in any case be considered as definitely and finally destroyed—it will be in our power. The despotism of capital, which is entirely in our hands, will hold out to it a straw, to which the state will be unavoidably compelled to cling; if it does not do so, it will inevitably fall into the abyss.

Of anybody who might, from motives of liberalism, be inclined to remark that discussions of this kind are immoral, I would ask the question, why is it not immoral for a state which has two enemies, one external and one internal, to use different means of defence against the former to that which it would use against the latter, to make secret plans of defence, to attack him by night or with superior forces? Why should it then be immoral for the state to use these means against that which ruins the foundations and welfare of its life?

"*Protocols of the Learned Elders of Zion*" is a total fabrication, depicting a supposed Jewish conspiracy to rule the entire world. Supposedly an actual "blueprint" for Jewish world domination, this book was first officially published in 1905. Millions have read it and it has changed the course of history. Millions continue to read it as actual fact, in spite of many governmental and literary sources stating that this book is a total hoax and fraud.

Can a sound and logical mind hope successfully to govern mobs by using arguments and reasoning, when there is a possibility of such arguments and reasonings being contradicted by other arguments, although these may possibly be ridiculous, but are made to appear more attractive to that portion of the populace which cannot think very deeply, guided as it is entirely by petty passions, habits, and conventions, and by sentimental theories? The uninitiated and ignorant populace, together with those who have risen from among them, get entangled in party dissensions which hinder all possibility of agreement even on a basis of sound arguments. Every decision of the masses is dependent on a chance or prearranged majority which, in its ignorance of political mysteries, passes absurd resolutions, thus sowing the germs of anarchy in the government.

Politics have nothing in common with morals. A ruler governed by morals is not a skilled politician, hence he is not firm on his throne. He who wants to rule must have recourse to cunningness and hypocrisy. The great human qualities of sincerity and honesty become vices in politics. They dethrone with more certainty than the bitterest enemy. These qualities have to be the attributes of the Gentile countries, but we are not in the least forced to be guided by them. Our right lies in might. The word "right" is an abstract idea established by nothing. This word signifies no more than "give me what I want in order to enable me to prove thereby that I am stronger than you are."

Where does "right" begin? Where does it end? In a state where power is badly organised, where the laws and the personality of the ruler are rendered inefficacious by the continual encroaching of liberalism, I take up a

A 2

This is also how communism works—to deceive the people!

Obviously, God's Chosen People were controlled by a higher power with morals!

The Jewish people have always prided themselves with the "might" of Almighty God!

This deception has caused the murders of many millions of "God's Chosen People."

Even Adolph Hitler used this book as a premise to killing over six million Jews. In the opinion of historian Norman Cohn, the *Protocols* was Hitler's primary justification for initiating the Holocaust--in his words: "his warrant for genocide."

new line of attack, making use of the right of might to destroy the existing rules and regulations, seize the laws, reorganise all the institutions, and thus become the dictator of those who, of their own free will, liberally renounced their power and conferred it on us. Our strength under the present shaky condition of the civil powers will be stronger than any other, because it will be invisible till the moment when it becomes so strong that no cunning designs will undermine it.

From the temporary evil, to which we are now obliged to have recourse, will emerge the benefit of an unshakable rule, which will reinstate the course of the mechanism of natural existence, which has been destroyed by liberalism. The end justifies the means. In making our plans we must pay attention not so much to what is good and moral, as to what is necessary and profitable.

We have in front of us a plan in which a strategic line is shown. From that line we cannot deviate unless we are going to destroy the work of centuries. To work out a suitable scheme of action one must bear in mind the meanness, instability, and want of ballast on the part of the crowd, its incapability to understand and respect the conditions of its own existence and of its own welfare. One must understand that the might of the crowd is blind and void of reason in discrimination, and that it lends its ear right and left. If the blind lead the blind, they will both fall together into the ditch. Consequently those members of the crowd who are upstarts from the people, even were they geniuses, cannot come forward as leaders of the mass without ruining the nation. Only a person brought up to autocratic sovereignty can read the words formed by political letters. The people abandoned to itself, *i.e.*, to upstarts from the masses, is ruined by party

We must remind ourselves that this entire book is a fraud. But the wording seems to suggest that the roots of communism are good, very contrary to the Jewish belief system.

From the Russian Czars to Iranian President Ahmadinejad, this one book has been their source for hatred of the Jews. Anti-Semitism's roots were planted with this one book. I cannot underscore how much damage this one supposed "literary work" has done to the Jews. It is incomprehensible and inconceivable how one fraudulent book can cause such disaster, mayhem, and outright carnage.

<u>This book is a lie</u>!

dissensions which arise from greed of power and honours and which create disturbances and disorder.

Is it possible for the mass to discriminate quietly, and without jealousies to administer the affairs of state, which they must not confuse with their personal interests? Can they be a defence against a foreign foe? This is impossible, as a plan broken up into as many parts as there are minds in the mass loses its value, and therefore becomes unintelligible and unworkable. Alone an autocrat can conceive vast plans clearly assigning its proper part to everything in the mechanism of the machine of state. Hence we conclude that it is expedient for the welfare of the country that the government of the same should be in the hands of one responsible person. Without absolute despotism civilisation cannot exist, for civilisation is capable of being promoted only under the protection of the ruler, whoever he may be, and not at the hands of the masses.

The crowd is a barbarian, and acts as such on every occasion. As soon as the mob has secured freedom it speedily turns it into anarchy, which in itself is the height of barbarism.

Just look at these alcoholised animals stupefied by the drink, of which unlimited use is tolerated by freedom! Should we allow ourselves and our fellow creatures to do likewise? The people of the Christians, bewildered by alcohol, their youths turned crazy by classics and early debauchery, to which they have been instigated by our agents, tutors, servants, governesses in rich houses, clerks, and so forth, by our women in places of their amusement—to the latter I add the so-called "society women"—their voluntary followers in corruption and luxury. Our motto must be "All means of force and hypocrisy."

* The original tenants of communism lean towards a complete dictatorship. Nothing of the sort is conceivable in the Jewish mindset.

Despotism is "a system of government in which the ruler has unlimited power" and will use ALL means to control the masses.

When reading *Protocols*, please always remember that it is a downright fraud. As we reflect on over one century of this infamous forgery, please understand that millions of our Jewish friends have died as a direct result of this deception.

Although we will delve into the history of this book, it was originally developed by the Russian Czar's secret police in 1900 - 1905. Its original claim supposedly is that it is the confidential minutes of a secret Jewish conclave in the last years of the 19th century. These world Jewish leaders, the "Elders of Zion," were supposedly conspiring to take over the world. This conspiratorial "secret plan for world domination" is quite unbelievable, even if one didn't know it was a proven fraud.

Even though the Israeli military is the finest in the world, the Jewish people are the most patient and peace-loving people you will ever meet!

Confiscation of property is one of the mainstays of communism. The Jewish people and communism are like mixing oil and water. It simply is impossible!

Only sheer force is victorious in politics, especially if it is concealed in the talent indispensable for statesmen. Violence must be the principle, cunning and hypocrisy must be the rule of those Governments which do not wish to lay down their crown at the feet of the agents of some new power. This evil is the only means of attaining the goal of good. Therefore, we must not stop short before bribery, deceit and treachery, if these are to serve the achievement of our cause.

In politics we must know how to confiscate property without any hesitation, if by so doing we can attain subjection and power. Our State, following the way of peaceful conquest, has the right of substituting for the terrors of war executions, less apparent and more expedient, which are necessary to uphold terror, producing blind submission. Just and implacable severity is the chief factor in State power. Not only for the sake of advantage, but also for that of duty and victory, we must keep to the programme of violence and hypocrisy. Our principles are as powerful as the means by which we put them into execution. That is why not only by these very means, but by the severity of our doctrines, we shall triumph and shall enslave all Governments under our super-Government. It suffices that it should be known that we are implacable in preventing recalcitrance. Even of old we were the first to cry out to the people, "Liberty, equality, and fraternity." Words so often repeated since that time by ignorant parrots flocking together from far and wide round these signposts; by repeating them they deprived the world of its prosperity and the individual of his real personal freedom, which formerly had been so well guarded from being choked by the mob.

The forgery contains numerous elements of what is known in literature as a "false document": a document that is deliberately written to fool the reader into believing that what is written is truthful and accurate even though, in actuality, it is not.

The *Protocols* tells of specific Jewish plans to subvert the morals of the non-Jewish world, plans for Jewish bankers to control the world's economies, plans for Jewish control of the press, and ultimately - plans for the destruction of civilization. The entire content is anti-Semitic. It is deep-rooted in frightened, conspiratorial, bigoted minds around the world, now especially amongst the Muslims.

7

The would-be wise and intelligent Gentiles did not discern how abstract were the words which they were uttering, and did not notice how little these words agreed with one another and even contradicted each other.

They did not see that in Nature there is no equality and that she herself created different and unequal standards of mind, character and capacity. It is likewise with the subjection to Nature's laws. These wiseacres did not divine that the mob is a blind power, and that the upstarts elected from its midst as rulers are likewise blind in politics; that a man intended to be a ruler, although a fool, can govern, but that a man who has not been so intended, although he might be a genius, would understand nothing of politics. All this was left out of sight by the Gentiles. At the same time, it was on this basis that dynastic rule was founded. The father used to instruct the son in the meaning and in the course of political evolutions in such a manner that no one except the members of the dynasty should have knowledge of it, and that none could disclose the secrets to the governed people. In time, the meaning of true political teachings as transmitted in dynasties from one generation to another was lost, and this loss contributed to the success of our cause. Our call of "Liberty, equality, and fraternity" brought whole legions to our ranks from all four corners of the world through our unconscious agents, and these legions carried our banners with ecstacy. In the meantime these words were eating, like so many worms, into the well being of the Christians and were destroying their peace, steadfastness and unity, thus ruining the foundations of the States. As we shall see later on, it was this action which brought about our triumph. It gave us the possibility among other things of playing the ace of

God intended for You to be a great ruler or leader. Please read 1 Timothy 3:1-7

It has been much heralded by anti-Semites as "written proof" that Jews are plotting to take over the entire world. But the anti-Semitism goes way beyond Stalin, Hitler, and other despots, it infiltrates young, impressionable minds even today.

Yes, *Protocols* is still a "best-seller" in spite of it being designated as a complete fraud. A new generation's minds have been poisoned by this anti-Semitic evil.

trumps—namely, the abolition of privileges; in other words, the existence of the Gentile aristocracy, which was the only protection nations and countries had against ourselves. On the ruins of natural and hereditary aristocracy we built an aristocracy of our own on a plutocratic basis.* We established this new aristocracy on wealth, of which we had control, and on science promoted by our scholars. Our triumph was rendered easier by the fact that we, through our connections with people who were indispensable to us, always worked upon the most susceptible part of the human mind, namely, by playing on our victims' weakness for profits, on their greed, on their insatiability, and on the material requirements of man; for each one of the said weaknesses, taken by itself, is capable of destroying initiative, thus handing over the will-power of the people to the mercy of those who would deprive them of all their power of initiative. The abstractness of the word "freedom" made it possible to convince the mob that the government is nothing else than a manager, representing the owner, that is to say, the nation, and can be discarded like a worn-out pair of gloves. The fact that the representatives of the nation can be deposed delivered these representatives into our power and practically put their appointment into our hands.

* I Timothy 6:10 teaches us that the LOVE of money is the root of all evil!

* * * * *

It is indispensable for our purpose that wars should not produce any territorial alterations. Thus, without territorial modifications, war would be transferred on to an economical footing. Then nations will recognise our superiority in the assistance which we shall render, and this state of affairs will put both sides at the mercy of our

Protocol #2 - talks about the Economic Wars

We can trace the roots of *Protocols* back to the mid-1800's. Under Napoleon III's reign in France, there was extreme enmity between France and Germany. Maurice Joly, a French attorney and writer, wrote very scathing communiqués on French politics. He was a severe denigrator of Napoleon III, deeming him a brutal despot. Wanting to reveal Napoleon's demonic plans, Maurice Joly wrote the book entitled *"The Dialogue in Hell Between Machiavelli and Montesquieu."* However, he committed suicide in Paris in 1878. Copies of his writings survived to influence future anti-Semitic writers.

international million-eyed agents, who are possessed of absolutely unlimited means. Then our international rights will sweep away the laws of the world and will rule countries in the same manner as individual governments rule their subjects.

We will select administrators from among the public, who will be possessed of servile tendencies. They will not be experienced in the art of government and therefore will be easily turned into pawns in our game in the hands of our learned and wise counsellors, who have been especially trained from early childhood for governing the world. As is already known to you, these men have studied the science of governing from our political plans, from experience of history and from observation of passing events. The Gentiles do not profit by continuous historical observations, but follow theoretical routine without contemplating what the results of the same may be. Therefore we need not take the Gentiles into consideration. Let them enjoy themselves until the time comes, or let them live in hopes of new amusements or on the reminiscences of passed joys. Let them think that these laws of theory, with which we have inspired them, are of supreme importance to them. With this object in view, and with the help of our press, we continually increase their blind faith in these laws. The educated classes of the Gentiles will pride themselves in their learning and, without verifying it, they will put into practice the knowledge obtained from science which was dished up to them by our agents with the object of educating their minds in the direction which we required.

Knowledge IS key. Hosea 4:6 says – "My children are destroyed for a lack of knowledge..."

Do not imagine that our assertions are empty words. Note here the success of Darwin, Marx and Nietsche prearranged by us. The demoralising effect of the tendencies

The crux of why this disastrous book was originally written was the Russian hatred towards the Jewish people, especially in the late 1890's. In 1894, Nicholas II was crowned Czar of Russia. He suppressed the Jews in many ways. In order to steer attention away from his own ineptness as a ruler, Nicholas II would blame the Jewish people for the troubles of the Russian empire. Eventually, he supported *pogroms* ("organized massacre of helpless people") against Jewish people.

Nicholas II was swayed by various strong opinions by his supposed "inner circle." Most of the time, he was oblivious to the mounting winds of revolution against the feudal system of the aristocracy and the czars. He continued to distrust Jews, but he did not know how to totally "handle them" except by force.

Protocols want to control your mind. God's Word says that He will grant you peace if your mind is fixed on Him!

of these sciences on the Gentile mind should certainly be obvious to us.

In order to refrain from making mistakes in our policy and administrative work, it is essential for us to study and bear in mind the present line of thought, the characters and tendencies of nations.

The triumph of our theory is its adaptability to the temperament of the nations with which we come in contact. It cannot be successful if its practical application is not based on the experience of the past in conjunction with observations of the present. The press in the hands of existing governments is a great power, by which the control of peoples' minds is obtained. The press demonstrates the vital claims of the populace, advertises complaints and sometimes creates discontent among the mob. The realisation of free speech is born in the press. But governments did not know how to make proper use of this power, and it fell into our hands. Through the press we achieved influence, although we ourselves kept in the background. Thanks to the press we accumulated gold, though it cost us streams of blood: it cost us the sacrifice of many of our people, but every sacrifice on our side is worth thousands of Gentiles before God.

* * * * *

Protocol #3 refers to the Methods of Conquest

To-day I can assure you that we are only within a few strides of our goal. There remains only a short distance and the cycle of the Symbolic Serpent—that badge of our people—will be complete. When this circle is locked, all the States of Europe will be enclosed in it, as it were, by unbreakable chains.

The existing constructional scales will soon collapse because we are continually throwing them out of balance

Much of Germany has been anti-Semitic for quite some time. The famous Petition of 1880 in Germany had over 265,000 signatures. This petition wanted to limit Jewish immigration, exclude Jews from high governmental positions, introduce a special census to keep track of Jews, and prohibit the hiring of Jews as elementary school teachers.

The *Protocols* brought together the religious, the social, and the political elements of ***Judeophobia*** in a very convincing manner. When it was first released, it expressed the resentment of the Christian world against the weakening of its faith and it sought to shut off public life to the Jews.

in order the more quickly to wear them out and destroy their effi ie ıcy.

The Gentiles thought that the scales had been made sufficiently strong and expected them to balance accurately. But the supporters of the scales—that is to say, the heads of States—are hampered by their servants who are of no avail to them, drawn away as they are by this unlimited power of intrigue which is theirs, thanks to the terrors prevailing in the palaces.

As the sovereign has no means of access to the hearts of his people, he cannot defend himself against the power-loving intriguers. As the watchful power has been separated by us from the blind power of the populace, b›th have lost their significance, because once parted they are as helpless as a blind man without a stick. In order to induce lovers of power to make a bad use of their rights, we set all powers one against the other by encouraging their liberal tendencies towards independence. We encouraged every undertaking in this direction; we placed formidable weapons in the hands of all parties and made power the goal of every ambition. Out of governments we made arenas on which party wars are fought out. Soon open disorder and bankruptcy will appear everywhere. Insuppressable babblers transformed parliamentary and administrative meetings into debating meetings. Audacious journalists and impudent pamphleteers are continually attacking the administrative powers. Abuse of power will definitely prepare the crash of all institutions and everything will fall prostrate under the blows of the raging populace. The people are enslaved in the sweat of their brows in poverty after a manner more formidable than the laws of serfdom. From the latter they could free themselves by some means or another,

Obviously this does not refer to the Jews—because our God is a God of peace and order.

A Universal Alliance of Israelites was organized in 1860 that sought to provide assistance for the targets of anti-Semitic oppression. It supported various educational activities and scholarly research projects, but it was never a real political force. It could offer little by way of answers when its enemies formed an International Anti-Semitic Congress in 1882 and supported what would become an inundation of hatred against Jews throughout Europe during the next two decades.

whereas nothing will liberate them from the tyranny of absolute want. We took care to insert rights in constitutions which for the masses are purely fictitious. All the so-called "rights of the people" can only exist in ideas which are not applicable in practice. How does it avail a workman of the proletariat, who is bent double by hard work and oppressed by his fate, if a chatterer gets the right to speak or a journalist the right to publish any kind of rubbish? What good is a constitution to the proletariat if they get no other advantage from it except the crumbs which we throw them from our table in return for their votes to elect our agents? Republican rights are an irony for the pauper, for the necessity of every day's labour keeps him from gaining any advantage by such rights and it only takes away the guarantee of continuous fixed wages, making him dependent on strikes, employers and comrades. Under our auspices the populace exterminated the aristocracy which had supported and guarded the people for its own benefit, which benefit is inseparable from the welfare of the populace. Nowadays, having destroyed the privileges of the aristocracy, the people fall under the yoke of cunning profiteers and upstarts.

One of our 10 Commandments says— THOU SHALL NOT KILL!

We intend to appear as though we were the liberators of the labouring man, come to free him from this oppression, when we shall suggest to him to join the ranks of our armies of Socialists, Anarchists and Communists. The latter we always patronise, pretending to help them out of fraternal principle and the general interest of humanity evoked by our socialistic masonry. The aristocracy, who by right shared the labour of the working classes, were interested in the same being well-fed, healthy and strong. We are interested in the opposite, *i.e.*, in the

Insider council members plotted to gain Nicholas's full attention by scheming to write a document which proved that the forbidden "modernization" of Russia was a Jewish plot, as untrue as this was.

degeneration of the Gentiles. Our strength lies in keeping the working man in perpetual want and impotence; because, by so doing, we retain him subject to our will and, in his own surroundings, he will never find either power or energy to stand up against us. Hunger will confer upon Capital more powerful rights over the labourer than ever the lawful power of the sovereign could confer upon the aristocracy.

Again, this does not pertain to the Jews. Jewish people are usually very successful businessmen, NOT bond-servants.

We govern the masses by making use of feelings of jealousy and hatred kindled by oppression and need. And by means of these feelings we brush aside those who impede us in our course.

When the time comes for our Worldly Ruler to be crowned, we will see to it that by the same means—that is to say, by making use of the mob—we will destroy everything that may prove to be an obstacle in our way.

The Gentiles are no longer capable of thinking without our aid in matters of science. That is why they do not realise the vital necessity of certain things, which we will make a point of keeping against the moment when our hour arrives—namely, that in schools the only true and the most important of all sciences must be taught, that is, the science of the life of man and social conditions, both of which require a division of labour and therefore the classification of people in castes and classes. It is imperative that every one should know that true equality cannot exist owing to the different nature of various kinds of work, and those who act in a manner detrimental to a whole caste have a different responsibility before the law to those who commit a crime only affecting their personal honour.

The true science of social conditions, to the secrets of which we do not admit the Gentiles, would convince the

In Russia, where anti-Semitism was "officially sponsored," Jacob Brafmann introduced the fable of a conspiracy through his two books, The Local and Universal Jewish Brotherhoods (1868) and The Book of the Kahal (1869). This "Jewish expert" for the governor general of the Northwest region of Russia saw the *kahal*, a form of self-government, as part of a vast network controlled by the Universal Alliance of Israelites. This network was supposedly worried about destabilizing Christian entrepreneurs, taking over all their property, and eventually seizing political power.

world that occupations and labour should be kept in specified castes so as not to cause human suffering, arising from an education which does not correspond with the work which individuals are called upon to do. If they were to study this science, the people would of their own free will submit to the ruling powers and to the castes of government classified by them. Under the present conditions of science and the line which we have allowed it to follow, the populace, in its ignorance, blindly believes in printed words and in erroneous illusions which have been duly inspired by us, and it bears malice to all classes which it thinks higher than itself. For it does not understand the importance of each caste. This hatred will become still more acute where economical crises are concerned, for then it will stop the markets and production. We will create a universal economical crisis, by all possible underhand means and with the help of gold, which is all in our hands. Simultaneously we will throw on to the streets huge crowds of workmen throughout Europe. These masses will then gladly throw themselves upon and shed the blood of those of whom, in their ignorance, they have been jealous from childhood, and whose belongings they will then be able to plunder.

They will not harm us, because the moment of the attack will be known to us and we will take measures to protect our interests.

We persuaded the Gentiles that liberalism would bring them to a kingdom of reason. Our despotism will be of this nature, for it will be in a position to put down all rebellions and by just severity to exterminate every liberal idea from all institutions.

When the populace noticed that it was being given all sorts of rights in the name of liberty, it imagined itself to

* How can there be hatred when our God is a God of love.

I Corinthians 13:13 says, "...but the greatest of these is love."

The anti-Semitic attitude was universal in its power. But nowhere was it more influential than in Russia. This nation was not only the most economically underdeveloped among what were known as "the great powers," but was also perhaps the most politically and culturally backward nation. Its culture was generally distrustful of liberal ideals and western individualism. Imperial Russia was controlled by a narrow-minded court and a medieval orthodox church. It was "the perfect storm setting" for the proclamation of the *Protocols*.

be the master, and tried to assume power. Of course, like every other blind man, the mass came up against innumerable obstacles. Then, as it did not wish to return to the former *régime*, it lay its power at our feet. Remember the French Revolution, which we call the "Great," the secrets of its preparatory organisation are well known to us, being the work of our hands. From that time onwards we have led nations from one disappointment to another, so that they should even renounce us in favour of the King-Despot of the blood of Zion, whom we are preparing for the world. At present we, as an international force, are invulnerable, because, whilst we are attacked by one Gentile government, we are upheld by others. In their intense meanness the Christian peoples help our independence—when kneeling they crouch before power; when they are pitiless towards the weak; merciless in dealing with faults and lenient to crimes; when they refuse to recognise the contradictions of freedom; when they are patient to the degree of martyrdom in bearing with the violence of an audacious despotism.

At the hands of their present dictators, premiers and ministers, they endure abuses, for the smallest of which they would have murdered twenty kings. How is this state of affairs to be explained? Why are the masses so illogical in their conception of events? The reason is, that despots persuade the people through their agents, that, although they may misuse their power and do injury to the state, this injury is done with a high purpose, *i.e.*, in order to attain prosperity for the populace, for the sake of international fraternity, unity and equality.

Certainly they do not tell them that such unification can only be obtained under our rule. So we see the populace condemning the innocent, and acquitting the

The Jews have never led any nation to any disappointment. You see, the Protocols turns truth upside down!

A shorter version of the Protocols actually appeared in 1903 in the newspaper *Znamia* (The Banner).

Sergei Nilus initially included the text in 1905 as an appendix to the second edition of his 1903 book entitled The Great in the Small: The Coming of the Anti-Christ and the Rule of Satan on Earth, which tells of his conversion from an experienced philosopher into a religious mystic. He was extremely eccentric.

guilty, convinced that it can always do what it pleases. Owing to this state of mind the mob destroys all solidity and creates disorder at every turn and corner. The word "liberty" brings society into conflict with all the powers, even with that of Nature and of God. That is why, when we come into power, we must strike the word "liberty" out of the human dictionary, as being the symbol of beastial power, which turns the populace into bloodthirsty animals. But we must bear in mind that these animals fall asleep as soon as they are satiated with blood, and at that moment it is easy to enchant and enslave them. If they are not given blood, they will not sleep, but will fight with one another.

* * * * *

Every republic passes through various stages. The first stage is the first days raging of the blind, sweeping and destroying right and left. The second, the reign of the demagogue, bringing forth anarchy and entailing despotism. This despotism is not officially legal, and, therefore, irresponsible; it is concealed and invisible, but, all the same, lets itself be felt. It is generally controlled by some secret organisation, which acts behind the back of some agent, and will, therefore, be the more unscrupulous and daring. This secret power will not mind changing its agents who mask it. The changes will even help the organisation, which will thus be able to rid itself of old servants, to whom it would have been necessary to pay larger bonuses for long service. Who or what can dethrone an invisible power? Now this is just what our government is. The masonic lodge throughout the world unconsciously acts as a mask for our purpose. But the use that we are going to make of this power in

Protocol #4 is the destruction of religion via materialism.

The so-called "Jewish Ritual" of Masonry is a delusion!

Paranoia has always been an element of anti-Semitism; and Nilus was no exception. He deemed every Jew a direct threat to him.

In his commentary to Protocols, he writes about the possibility of the Jews bringing forth the Anti-christ. He writes: "There is no room left for doubt. With all the might and terror of Satan, the reign of the triumphant King of Israel is approaching our unregenerate world; the King born of the blood of Zion - the Anti-christ - is near to the throne of universal power."

our plan of action, and even our headquarters, remain perpetually unknown to the world at large.

Liberty could be harmless and exist in governments and countries without being detrimental to the welfare of the people, if it were based on religion and fear of God, on human fraternity, free from ideas of equality, which are in direct contradiction to the laws of creation, and which have ordained submission.

Governed by such a faith as this, the people would be ruled under the guardianship of their parishes, and would exist quietly and humbly under the guidance of the spiritual pastor, and submit to God's disposition on earth. That is why we must extract the very conception of God from the minds of the Christians and replace it by arithmetical calculations and material needs. In order to divert the minds of the Christians from our policy, it is essential that we should keep them occupied with trade and commerce. Thus all nations will be striving for their own profits, and in this universal struggle will not notice their common enemy. But, so that liberty should entirely dislocate and ruin the social life of the Gentiles, we must put commerce on a speculative basis. The result of this will be, that the riches of the land extracted by production will not remain in the hands of the Gentiles, but will pass through speculation into our coffers.

The struggle for superiority and continuous speculations in the business world will create a demoralised, selfish and heartless society. This society will become completely indifferent and even disgusted by religion and politics. Lust of gold will be their only guide. And this society will strive after this gold, making a veritable cult of the materialistic pleasures with which it can keep them supplied. Then the lower classes will join us against our

B

It is virtually impossible to EXTRACT the concept of God from our minds. Scriptures say that He has given to you "A SOUND MIND."

Quite the contrary, money does come to the Jews and the lover of Jews!

Sergei Nilus, a Russian Orthodox Christian, supported the Czars. At one point he worked as a clerical official for the Russian Secret Police. As the czars began to lose the control and loyalty of the Russian people, the Secret Police became more alert to what was really going on. They felt that an anti-Jewish document might "take the heat off" the ruling czars. They greatly encouraged Nilus. Other conservative and anti-democratic forces would readily accept this writing of hatred, like the Black Hundreds, a secret nationalistic organization and strong pro-active, anti-Semitic group.

competitors—the privileged Gentiles—with no pretence to a noble motive, or even for the sake of riches, but out of pure hatred towards the upper classes.

* * * * *

Protocol # 5 –
DESPOTISM AND MODERN PROGRESS

What kind of government can one give to societies in which bribery and corruption have penetrated everywhere, where riches can only be obtained by cunning surprises and fraudulent means, in which dissensions continuously prevail; where morality must be supported by punishment and strict laws, and not by voluntary accepted principles, in which patriotic and religious feelings are merged in cosmopolitan convictions?

What form of government can be given to these societies other than the despotic form, which I will describe to you?

A "despot" is a ruler with absolute power and authority. These lines refer to either communism or socialism, NOT "God's Chosen People!"

We will organise a strong centralised government, so as to gain social powers for ourselves. By new laws we will regulate the political life of our subjects, as though they were so many parts of a machine. Such laws will gradually restrict all freedom and liberties allowed by the Gentiles. Thus our reign will develop into such a mighty despotism, that it will be able at any time or place to squash discontented or recalcitrant Gentiles.

We shall be told that the kind of despotism which I suggest will not suit the actual progress of civilisation, but I will prove to you that the contrary is the case. In the days when the people looked on their sovereigns as on the will of God, they quietly submitted to the despotism of their monarchs. But from the day that we inspired the populace with the idea of its own rights, they began to regard kings as ordinary mortals. In the eye of the mob the holy anointment fell from the head of monarchs, and, when we took away their religion, the power was

Nilus had several spurious versions of how he acquired the supposed information. One story that he originally told says that he obtained this information from a person who said he had stolen it from (non-existent) Zionist archives in Paris.

thrown into the streets like public property, and was snatched up by us. Moreover, among our administrative gifts, we count also that of ruling the masses and individuals by means of cunningly constructed theories and phraseology, by rules of life and every other kind of device. All these theories, which the Gentiles do not at all understand, are based on analysis and observation, combined with so skilful a reasoning as cannot be equalled by our rivals, any more than these can compete with us in the construction of plans for political actions and solidarity. The only society known to us which would be capable of competing with us in these arts, might be that of the Jesuits. But we have managed to discredit these in the eyes of the stupid mob as being a palpable organisation, whereas we ourselves have kept in the background, reserving our organisation as a secret.

Moreover, what difference will it make to the world who is to become its master, whether the head of the Catholic Church, or a despot of the blood of Zion?

But to us, "the Chosen People," the matter cannot be indifferent. For a time the Gentiles might perhaps be able to deal with us. But on this account we need fear no danger, as we are safeguarded by the deep roots of their hatred for one another, which cannot be extracted.

We set at variance with one another all personal and national interests of the Gentiles, by promulgating religious and tribal prejudices among them, for nearly twenty centuries. To all this, the fact is due that not one single government will find support from its neighbours when it calls upon them for it, in opposing us, because each one of them will think that action against us might be disastrous for its individual existence. We are too

Protocols is the "Bible" of anti-Semitism!

The Jews ARE "Chosen People"

Another story is that he got them from the first Zionist Congress in Basel, 1897, led by Theodor Herzl. However, that first Zionist Congress was NOT a *secret* meeting that Nilus claimed it was. Even the minutes of that meeting were published openly. So he had to change his story again.

powerful—the world has to reckon with us. Governments cannot make even a small treaty without our being secretly involved in it. "Per me reges regunt"—let kings reign through me. We read in the Law of the Prophets that we have been chosen by God to rule the earth. God gave us genius, in order that we should be capable of performing this work. Were there a genius in the enemy's camp he might yet fight us, but a newcomer would be no match for old hands like ourselves, and the struggle between us would be of such a desperate nature as the world has never yet seen. It is already too late for their genius. All the wheels of state-mechanism are set in motion by a power, which is in our hands, that is to say—gold.

The science of political economy, thought out by our learned scientists, has already proved that the power of capital is greater than the prestige of the Crown.

Capital, in order to have a free field, must obtain absolute monopoly of trade and commerce. This is already being achieved by an invisible hand in all parts of the world. Such a freedom will give political power to traders, who, by profiteering, will oppress the populace.

Protocols display a blatant hatred and animosity towards the Jews!

Nowadays it is more important to disarm the people than to lead them to war. It is more important to use burning passions for our cause, than to extinguish them; to encourage the ideas of others and use them for our own purpose, than to dissipate them. The main problem for our government is: how to weaken the brain of the public by criticism, how to make it lose its power of reasoning, which creates opposition, and how to distract the public mind by senseless phraseology.

At all times nations, as well as individuals, have taken words for deeds, as they are contented with what they

God has told us that the use of "idle words" is a sin.

The *Protocols* was probably obtained by Nilus from the director of the foreign branch of the Russian secret police named Piotor Rachovsky, who was always interested in promoting himself. Since Nilus was a clerk with the Russian Secret Police, he surely had unparalleled access to the supposed Protocols.

hear, and seldom notice whether the promise has been actually fulfilled. Therefore, simply for the purpose of show, we will organise institutions, members of which, by eloquent speeches, will prove and praise their contributions to "progress."

We will assume a liberal appearance for all parties and for all tendencies, and will provide all our orators with one. These orators will be so loquacious, that they will weary the people with speeches to such a degree, that the people will have more than enough of oratory of any kind.

In order to secure public opinion, this must first be made utterly confused by the expression from all sides of all manner of contradictory opinions, until the Gentiles become lost in their labyrinth. Then they will understand that the best course to take is to have no opinion on political matters—matters which are not intended to be understood by the public, but which should only be reserved to the directors of affairs. This is the first secret.

The second secret, necessary for our successful governing, consists in multiplying to such an extent the faults, habits, passions, and conventional laws of the country, that nobody will be able to think clearly in the chaos—therefore men will cease to understand one another.

This policy will also help us to sow dissensions amongst all parties, to dissolve all collective powers, and to discourage all individual initiative, which might in any way hinder our schemes.

There is nothing more dangerous than personal initiative: if there are brains at the back of it, it may do more harm to us than the millions of people whom we have set at one another's throats.

God's people are not confused. "Where there is no revelation the people cast off restraint." - Proverbs 29:18

"May the God who gives endurance and encouragement give YOU the spirit of UNITY among yourselves as you follow Christ Jesus." - Romans 15:5 (NIV)

Other stories by Nilus simply did not hold up to scholarly scrutiny by learned men in Europe. It was originally seen as an effort to help defend the czarist regime. Despite originally embracing this scurrilous work, the Czar eventually labeled it as *"anti-Semitic propaganda."* It was later confiscated; but the damage had already been done.

God tells us that who the Son sets free—is FREE INDEED! That means NO oppression!

We must direct the education of Christian societies in such a way, that in all cases where initiative is required for an enterprise, their hands should drop in hopeless despair. Tension, brought about by freedom of action, loses force when it encounters the freedom of others. Hence come—moral shocks, disappointments and failures. By all these means we will so oppress the Christians that they will be forced to ask us to govern them internationally. When we attain such a position we shall be able, straightway, to absorb all powers of governing throughout the whole world, and to form a universal Supergovernment. In the place of existing governments we will place a monster, which will be called the Administration of the Supergovernment. Its hands will be outstretched like far-reaching pinchers, and it will have such an organisation at its disposal, that it will not possibly be able to fail in subduing all countries. Soon we will start organising great monopolies—reservoirs of colossal wealth, in which even the large fortunes of the Gentiles will be involved to such an extent that they will sink together with the credit of their government the day after the political crisis takes place.*

Protocol # 6 - Takeover Technique!

Those among you who are present here to-day, and are economists, just calculate the importance of this scheme!

We must use every possible kind of means to develop the popularity of our Supergovernment, holding it up as a protection and recompenser of all who willingly submit to us.

The aristocracy of the Gentiles, as a political power, is no more,—therefore we need not consider it any more from

* It being evidently intended that the Jews should withdraw their money at the last moment.

Even Nilus reportedly believed he might be working with a forgery. However, this did not stop him. He felt he was responsible for saving Russia from attack from within the country, as well as attacks from other countries.

that point of view. But as landowners they are still dangerous to us, because their independent existence is ensured through their resources. Therefore it is essential for us, at all costs, to deprive the aristocracy of their lands. To attain this purpose the best method is to force up rates and taxes. These methods will keep the landed interests at their lowest possible ebb. The aristocrats of the Gentiles, who, by the tastes which they have inherited, are incapable of being contented with a little, will soon be ruined.

At the same time we must give all possible protection to trade and commerce, and especially to speculation, the principal *rôle* of which is to act as a counterpoise to industry.

Without speculation industry will enlarge private capitals and will tend to raise agriculture by freeing the land from debt and mortgages, advanced by agricultural banks. It is essential that industry should drain the land of all its riches,and speculation should deliver all the world's wealth thus procured into our hands. By this means all the Gentiles would be thrown into the ranks of the proletariat. Then the Gentiles will bow down before us, in order to obtain the right to exist.

In order to ruin the industry of the Gentiles and to help speculation, we will encourage the love for boundless luxury, which we have already developed. We will increase the wages, which will not help the workmen, as at the same time we will raise the price of prime necessities, taking as a pretext the bad results of agriculture. We will also artfully undermine the basis of production by sowing seeds of anarchy amongst the workmen, and encouraging them in the drinking of spirits. At the same time we will use all possible means to drive

What a greater example of communism or communal socialism.

The Protocols provides a motivation to action and a justification for violence; which is NOT Jewish!

Sergei Nilus was not concerned with writing the truth. He just wanted people to support his anti-Semitic ideas.

When compared side-by-side with Joly's "*Dialogue,*" it was obvious there were tremendous amounts of plagiarism. The London Times on August 17, 1921 exposed the historic "FAKE" of the Protocols. However, now even more people wanted to buy the fraud!

He died of heart failure on January 14, 1929 at the age of 67.

all the Gentile intelligence from the land. In order that the true position of affairs should not be prematurely realised by the Gentiles, we will conceal it by an apparent desire to help the working classes in solving great economical problems, the propaganda of which our economical theories are assisting in every possible way.

* * * *

Protocol #7 - WORLDWIDE WARS

Intensified military service and the increase of the police force are essential to complete the above mentioned plans. It is essential for us to arrange that, besides ourselves, there should be in all countries nothing but a huge proletariat, so many soldiers and police loyal to our cause.

In the whole of Europe, and with the help of Europe, we must promote on other continents sedition, dissensions and mutual hostility. In this there is a twofold advantage: firstly by these means we command the respect of all countries, who well know that we have the power to create upheavals at will, or else to restore order. All countries are used to look to us for the necessary pressure, when such is required. Secondly, by intrigues we shall entangle all the threads spun by us in the ministries of all governments not only by our politics, but by trade conventions and financial obligations.

An ongoing, myth of hatred!

In order to obtain these ends we must have recourse to much slyness and artfulness during negotiations and agreements, but in what is called "official language" we shall assume the opposite tactics of appearing honest and amenable. Thus the governments of the Gentiles, which we taught to look only on the showy side of affairs, as we present these to them, will even look upon us as benefactors and saviours of humanity.

Judeophobia was an intricate part of the "political fabric" of Russia when the *Protocols* first appeared.

Behind the scenes, Nicholas and Alexandra encouraged the Black Hundreds anti-Semitic cult. They initially supported the Protocols without reservation. They ordered a sermon quoting the Protocols in all the 368 churches of Moscow. They also supported its publication in right-wing newspapers. They used the Protocols to deflect criticism against them, by claiming the Jews had inspired the massive strikes in Russia.

We must be in a position to meet every opposition with a declaration of war on the part of the neighbouring country of that state which dares to stand in our way; but if such neighbours in their turn were to decide to unite in opposing us, we must respond by creating a universal war.

The main success in politics consists in the degree of secrecy employed in pursuing it. The action of a diplomat must not correspond with his words. To help our world-wide plan, which is nearing its desired end, we must influence the governments of the Gentiles by so-called public opinions, in reality prearranged by us by means of that greatest of all powers—the press, which, with a few insignificant exceptions not worth taking into account, is entirely in our hands.

Briefly, in order to demonstrate our enslavement of the Gentile governments in Europe, we will show *our power to one of them by means of crimes of violence*, that is to say by *a reign of terror*;* and in case they all rise against us we will respond with American, Chinese or Japanese guns.

* * * * *

We must secure all instruments which our enemies might turn against us. We shall have recourse to the most intricate and complicated expressions of the dictionary of law in order to acquit ourselves in case we are forced to give decisions, which may seem overbold and unjust. For it will be important to express such decisions in so forcible a manner, that they should seem to the populace to be of the highest moral, equitable and just nature. Our government must be surrounded by all the powers of civilisation among which it will have to act. It will draw

* Note the present state of Russia.

Protocols indicate a "warrant for genocide!"

Protocol # 8 - is a TRANSITIONAL GOVERNMENT.

They even used the Protocols as a form of self-rationalization for their dreadful theocratic government and the defeats it experienced in the Russian Revolution of 1905.

Even after they learned that the Protocols was a fraud, they granted funding for publishing the documents.

to itself publicists, lawyers, practitioners, administrators, diplomats, and finally people prepared in our special advanced schools. These people will know the secrets of social life; they will master all languages put together by political letters and words; they will be well acquainted with the inner side of human nature, with all its most sensitive strings, on which they will have to play. These strings form the construction of the Gentile brain, their good and bad qualities, their tendencies and vices, the peculiarity of castes and classes. Of course these wise counsellors of our might to whom I allude will not be selected from amongst the Gentiles, who are used to carry on their administrative work without bearing in mind the results which they have to achieve, and without knowing for what purpose these results are required. The administrators of the Gentiles sign papers without reading them, and serve for love of money or ambition.

Another lie!

God commands us to "BE DILIGENT!"

His Word promises that "the wealth of the wicked will be stored up for the righteous!"

We will surround our government by a whole host of economists. That is the reason why science of economy is the principal subject taught to the Jews. We will be surrounded by thousands of bankers, traders, and, what is still more important, by millionaires, because in reality everything will be decided by money. Meanwhile, as long as it is not yet safe to fill government posts with our brother Jews, we will entrust these important posts to people whose record and characters are so bad as to form a gulf between the nation and themselves, and to such people who, in case they disobey our orders, may expect judgment and imprisonment. And all this is with the object that they should defend our interests until the last breath has passed out of their bodies.

Applying our principles, pay special attention to the character of the particular nation, by which you are

More than 100 *pogroms* (in truth—massacres!) occurred between 1903 and 1906 against the Jewish people in Russia. There were more than 5,000 Jewish deaths in more than 53 cities and 600 villages in 1905 alone.

surrounded and amongst which you have to work. You must not expect to be successful in applying our principles all round until the nation in question has been re-educated by our doctrines; but by proceeding carefully in the application of our principles you will discover that, before ten years have elapsed, the most stubborn character will have changed and we shall have added yet another nation to the ranks of those who have already submitted to us.

For the liberal words of our masonic motto, " fr.edom, equality, and fraternity," we will substitute not the words of our motto, but words expressing simply an idea, and we will say "the right of freedom, the duty of equality, and the idea of fraternity," and we shall have the bull by the horns. As a matter of fact we have already destroyed all ruling powers except our own, but in theory they still exist. At the present time, if any governments make themselves objectionable to us, it is only a formality, and undertaken with our full knowledge and consent, as we need their anti-Semitic outbursts in order to enable us to keep our small brothers in order. I will not enlarge upon this point, for it has alrcady formed the subject of many discussions.

As a matter of fact we are encountered by no opposition. Our government is in so exceedingly strong a position in the sight of the law that we may almost describe it by the powerful expression of dictatorship. I can honestly say that at the present time we are legislators, we sit in judgment and inflict punishments, we execute and pardon, we are, as it were, the commander-in-chief of all armies, riding at their head. We rule by mighty force, because in our hands remain the fragments of a once powerful party, now under our subjection. We possess boundless

The truth shall set you FREE! (John 8:32)

We come against powers and principalities!

Anti-Semitism was of epidemic proportions in Russia; even more than in Germany. Between 1905 and 1906, Russia published over 14 million copies of approximately 3,000 anti-Semitic books and pamphlets with the czar himself contributing over 12 million rubles to the enterprise.

ambitions, *devouring greed, merciless revenge and intense hatred.* We are the source of a far-reaching terror. We employ in our service people of all opinions and all parties: men desiring to reestablish monarchies, socialists, communists, and supporters of all kinds of utopias. We have put them all into harness; each one of them in his own way undermines the remnant of power and tries to destroy all existing laws. By this procedure all governments are tormented, they yell for rest and, for the sake of peace, are prepared to make any sacrifice. But we will not give them any peace until they humbly recognise our international super-government.

Protocols call for a One World Government.

The populace clamoured for the necessity of solving the social problem by international means. Dissensions among parties handed these over to us, because in order to conduct an opposition money is essential, and money is under our control.

We have feared the alliance of the experienced Gentile sovereign power with that of the blind power of the mob, but all measures to prevent the possibility of such an occurrence have been taken by us. Between these two powers we have erected a wall in the form of the terror which they entertain for one another. Thus the blind power of the populace remains a support on our side. We alone will be its leaders, and will guide it towards the attainment of our object. In order that the hand of the blind should not free itself from our grip, we must be in constant contact with the masses if not personally, at any rate through our most faithful brothers. When we become a recognised power we will personally address the populace in the market places, and will instruct it in political matters in whatever direction may suit our convenience.

Historian Stephen Eric Bronner writes: "The Russian Revolution was followed in 1918 by the start of a brutal civil war in which the republican option vanished: it created the need for a simple choice between Reds and Whites. Most Jews sought only peace and an escape from a conflict whose barbarity was extreme even by the standards of the day. When forced to choose the lesser evil, however, most supported the Bolsheviks against the staunchly anti-Semitic Whites."

How are we to verify what the people are taught in country schools? But it is certain that what is said by the envoy of the government, or by the sovereign himself, cannot fail to be known to the whole nation, as it is soon spread by the voice of the people.

In order not to destroy the institutions of the Gentiles prematurely, we reached them with our experienced hand and secured the ends of the springs in their mechanism. The latter formerly were in severe but just order; for them we have substituted disorderly liberal management. We have had a hand in jurisdiction, electioneering, in the management of the press, in furthering the liberty of the individual, and, what is still more important, in education, which constitutes the main support of free existence.

We have befooled and corrupted the rising generation of the Gentiles by educating them in principles and theories known to us to be thoroughly false, but which we ourselves have inculcated. Without actually amending the laws already in force, but by simply distorting them and by placing interpretations upon them which were not intended by those who framed them, we have obtained an extraordinarily useful result.

These results became at first apparent by the fact that our interpretation concealed the real meaning of the laws, and subsequently rendered them so unintelligible that it was impossible for the government to disentangle such a confused code of laws.

Hence the theory arose of not adhering to the letter of the law, but of judging by conscience. It is contended that nations can rise in arms against us if our plans are discovered prematurely; but in anticipation of this we can rely upon throwing into action such a formidable force

"Because you have rejected knowledge, I also will reject you from being priest for me." Hosea 4:6b

Not the letter of the law, but the SPIRIT of the law gives light!

"This, in turn, only confirmed the belief perpetrated by new editions of the Protocols that the Jews were behind both the bourgeois provisional government, supported by liberals and socialists, and the proletarian dictatorship. The two phases of the revolution had seemingly become one and, viewing the Jews as solidifying the connection between them, the Protocols provided the extreme right with a way of explaining in its own terms what Trotsky called 'the permanent revolution'."

Perfect love casts out fear (1 John 4:18)

Protocol #6 - PREPARING FOR POWER

In the last days, God's Word says: "Men shall be lovers of pleasure rather than lovers of God." (2 Timothy 3:4)

as will make even the bravest of men shudder. By then metropolitan railways and underground passages will be constructed in all cities. From these subterranean places we will explode all the cities of the world, together with their institutions and documents.*

* * * * *

To-day I will begin by repeating what has been previously mentioned, and I beg all of you to bear in mind that in politics, governments and nations are satisfied by the showy side of everything; yes, and how should they have time to examine the inner side of things when their representatives only think of amusements?

It is most important for our politics to bear in mind the above-mentioned detail, as it will be of great help to us, when discussing such questions as the distribution of power, freedom of speech, freedom for the press and religion, rights of forming associations, equality in the sight of the law, inviolability of property and domicile, the question of taxation (idea of secret taxation) and the retrospective force of laws. All similar questions are of such a nature that it is not advisable to openly discuss them in front of the populace. But in cases where it is imperative that these should be mentioned to the mob they must not be enumerated but, without going into detail, statements should be made concerning the principles of modern right as recognised by us. The importance of reticence lies in the fact that a principle which has not been openly declared leaves us freedom of action, whereas such a principle, once declared, becomes as good as established.

The nation holds the power of a political genius in special respect and endures all its high-handed actions, and

* Probably figurative, referring to such means as Bolshevism.

These outright forgeries have played a large part behind-the-scenes in assisting the anti-Bolshevist response in Russia, which had occupied so much of the public mindset during the critical years of 1919-1921.

thus regards them: "What a dirty trick, but how skilfully executed!" "What a swindle, but how well and with what courage it has been done!"

We count on attracting all nations to work on the construction of the foundations of the new edifice which has been planned by us. For this reason it is necessary for us to acquire the services of bold and daring agents, who will be able to overcome all obstacles in the way of our progress.

When we accomplish our *coup d'état*, we will say to the people: "Everything has been going very badly; all of you have suffered; now we are destroying the cause of your sufferings, that is to say, nationalities, frontiers and national currencies. Certainly you will be free to condemn us, but can your judgment be fair if you pronounce it before you have had experience of what we can do for your good?"

Then they will carry us shoulder high in triumph, in hope and in exultation. Power of voting, in which we trained the most insignificant members of mankind by organising meetings and prearranged agreements, will then play its last part; this power, by the means of which we have "enthroned ourselves," will discharge its last debt to us in its anxiety to see the outcome of our proposition before pronouncing its judgment.

The Protocols remains one of the most infamous documents ever written!

In order to obtain an absolute majority we must induce everybody to vote, without discriminating between classes. Such a majority would not be obtained from educated classes or from a society divided into castes.

Having then inspired every man's mind with the idea of his own self-importance, we will destroy the family life of the Gentiles and its educational importance; we will prevent men with clever brains from coming to the front,

Lenin, Trotsky, and their associates were not only extreme Communists, but were also avowed atheists. The great bulk of the Jews in Russia were extremely orthodox members of the Synagogue, who hold in revulsion every sign of atheism. In their economic affiliation these Jews were no less hostile to Bolshevism. They belonged in an overwhelming proportion to the upper and middle-class bourgeoisie.

The Jews—YOU and I—we are not a * "mob".

We were individually created in the image and likeness of God!

and such men the populace, under our guidance, will keep subdued and will not permit them even to state their plans.

* The mob is used to listen to us, who pay it for its attention and obedience. By these means we shall create such a blind force that it will never be capable of taking any decision without the guidance of our agents, placed by us for the purpose of leading them.

The mob will submit to this system, because it will know that from these leaders will depend its wages, earnings, and all other benefits. The system of government must be the work of one head, because it will be impossible to consolidate it, if it is the combined work of numerous minds. That is why we are only allowed to know the plan of action, but must by no means discuss it in order not to destroy its efficacy, the functions of its separate parts and the practical meaning of each point. If such plans were to be discussed and altered by repeated submissions at the polls, they would be distorted by the results of all mental misunderstandings, which arise owing to the voters not having fathomed the depth of their meanings. Therefore, it is necessary that our plans should be decisive and logically thought out. That is the reason why we must not throw the great work of our leader to be torn to pieces by the mob, or even by a small clique. For the present these plans will not upset existing institutions. They will only alter their theory of economy, and therefore all their course of procedures, which will then inevitably follow the way prescribed by our plans. In all countries there exist the same institutions only under different names: the houses of representatives of the people, the ministries, the senate, a privy council of sorts, legislative and administrative departments.

Following the Russian Revolution in 1917, exasperated supporters of the overthrown Czar salvaged the document from obscurity in order to discredit the Bolsheviks. The émigré Czarists portrayed the Revolution as part of a Jewish plot to enslave the world, and pointed to the *Protocols* as the "Blueprint" for that plan.

I need not explain to you the connecting mechanism of these different institutions, as it is already well known to you. Only note that each of the above-mentioned institutions corresponds to some important function of the government. (I use the word "important" not with reference to the institutions, but with reference to their functions.)

All these institutions have divided among themselves all functions of government, that is to say, administrative, legislative, and executive powers. And their functions have become similar to those of the divers separate organs of the human body.

If we injure any part of the government machinery, the state will fall sick as a human body and will die. When we injected the poison of liberalism into the organism of the state its political complexion changed; the states became infected with a mortal illness, that is, decomposition of the blood. There remains only to await the end of their agonies. Liberalism gave birth to constitutional governments, which took the place of autocracy—the only wholesome form of government for the Gentiles. Constitution, as you know for yourselves, is nothing more than a school for dissensions, disagreements, quarrels, and useless party agitations; in brief, it is the school of everything that weakens the efficiency of the government. The tribune, as well as the Press, has tended to make the rulers inactive and weak, thus rendering them useless and superfluous, and for this reason they were deposed in many countries.

Then the institution of a republican era became possible; and then, in the place of the sovereign, we put a caricature of the same in the person of a president, whom we chose from the mob from among our creatures and our slaves.

C

Autocracy – a government in which one person has absolute power.

Remember—

Protocols is a total LIE!

Leonard Trotsky called the 1905 Russian Revolution the "dress rehearsal" for 1917 communist takeover.

Karl Marx, the architect of communism via his work, the Communist Manifesto, was often thought of as a Jew by right-wing anti-Semites who wanted to see the Russian revolution as part of the Jewish global conspiracy.

Thus we laid the mine which we have placed under the Gentiles, or rather under the Gentile nations. In the near future we will make the president a responsible person.

Then we will have no scruples in boldly applying the plans, for which our own "dummy" will be responsible. What does it matter to us if the ranks of place-hunters become weak, if confusions arise from the fact that a president cannot be found—confusions which will definitely disorganise the country?

In order to achieve these results, we will prearrange for the election of such presidents, whose past record is marked with some "Panama" scandal or other shady hidden transaction. A president of such a kind will be a faithful executor of our plans, as he will fear denouncement, and will be under the influence of the fear which always possesses a man who has attained power and is anxious to retain the privileges and honours associated with his high office. The House of Representatives will elect, protect, and screen the president; but we will deprive this House of its power of introducing and altering laws.

Absolute power does corrupt!

God commands us to pray for our leaders in government!

This power we will give to the responsible president, who will be a mere puppet in our hands. In that case the power of the president will become a target exposed to various attacks, but we will give him means of defence in his right of appeal to the people above the heads of the representatives of the nation, that is to say, direct to the people, who are our blind slaves—the majority of the mob.

Moreover, we will empower the president to proclaim martial law. We will explain this prerogative by the fact that the president, being head of the army, must

Marx's materialistic and anti-religious worldview was permeated with anti-Semitism of the worst kind. Since his enemy was capitalism, and the power of property was seen as the characteristic iniquity of the world, the definitive anti-Semitic theme of the Jews as greedy money-lenders was not adopted by him. He wrote: "Let us not seek the secret of the Jew in his religion, but let us seek the secret of religion in the real Jew." He viewed the Jew as an enemy of mankind, and especially of communism.

have the same under his command for the protection of the new republican constitution, which protection is his duty as its responsible representative.

Of course, under such conditions, the key of the inner position will be in our hands, and none other than ourselves will control legislation.

Moreover, when we introduce the new republican constitution, we will, under pretext of state secrecy, deprive the house of its right of questioning the desirability of measures taken by the Government. By this new constitution we will also reduce the number of the representatives of the nation to a minimum, thus also reducing an equivalent number of political passions, and passion for politics. If, in spite of this, they should become recalcitrant, we will abolish the remaining representatives by appealing to the nation. It will be the President's prerogative to appoint the chairman and vice-chairman of the house of representatives and of the senate. In place of continuous sessions of parliaments we will institute sessions of a few months' duration. Moreover, the president, as head of the executive power, will have the right to convene or dissolve parliament and, in case of dissolution, to defer the convocation of a new parliament. But, in order that the president should not be held responsible for the consequences of these, strictly speaking, illegal acts, before our plans have matured, we will persuade the Ministers and other high administrative officials, who surround the president, to circumvent his orders by issuing instructions of their own and thus compel them to bear the responsibility instead of the President. This function we would especially recommend to be allotted to the senate, to the council of state, or to the cabinet, but not to individuals. Under our guidance the President will

God's law has order. We are to obey the laws of the land. Therefore, this cannot be a Jewish trait, either!

Marx wrote in his book, The Capacity, his definitive anti-Semitic solution to the Jewish problem: "In the final analysis, the emancipation of the Jews is the emancipation of mankind from Judaism."

36

interpret laws, which might be understood in several ways.

Moreover he will annul laws in cases when we consider this to be desirable. He will also have the right to propose new temporary laws and even modifications in the constitutional work of the government, using as a motive for so doing the exigencies of the welfare of the country.

Such measures will enable us to gradually withdraw any rights and indulgences that we may have been forced to grant when we first assumed power. Such indulgences we will have to introduce in the constitution of governments in order to conceal the gradual abolition of all constitutional rights, when the time comes to change all existing governments for our autocracy. The recognition of our autocrat may possibly be realised before the abolition of constitutions, namely, the recognition of our rule will start from the very moment when the people, torn by dissensions and smarting under the insolvency of their rulers (which will have been pre-arranged by us), will yell out: "Depose them, and give us one world-ruler, who could unify us and destroy all causes of dissension, namely, frontiers, nationalities, religions, state debts, etc. . . . a ruler who could give us peace and rest, which we cannot find under the government of our sovereigns and representatives."

But you know full well for yourselves that, in order that the multitude should yell for such a request, it is imperative in all countries to continually disturb the relationship which exists between people and governments. —hostilities, wars, hatred, and even martyrdom with hunger and need, and with the inoculation of diseases, to such an extent, that the Gentiles should not see any exit

Governing by "fiat" or by Executive Orders only—will help to bring down any government.

There it is again—a One World Government! BEWARE!

James 1:8 says: A double-minded man is unstable in all his ways.

The pogroms in the Ukraine and the Crimea were directly influenced by the advent of the *Protocols*. The pogroms' outcome was horrific. Jewish casualties during the civil war numbered around 330,000. Somehow, no one seems to remember just how horrible this massacre really was—all because of the *Protocols*.

from their troubles other than an appeal for the protection of our money and for our complete sovereignty.

But if we give the nation time to take breath, another such opportunity would be hardly likely to recur.

The council of state will accentuate the power of the ruler. In its capacity as an official legislative body it will be, as it were, a committee for issuing the rulers' commands.

Here then is a programme of the new constitution, which we are preparing for the world. We will make laws, define constitutional rights, and administer such by means of (1) edicts of the legislative chamber, suggested by the president; (2) by means of general orders and orders of the senate and state council, and by means of decisions of the cabinet; and (3) when the opportune moment presents itself, by the means of a *coup d'état.*

Thus, having roughly determined our plan of action, we will discuss such details as may be necessary for us to accomplish the revolution in the sets of wheels of the state mechanism in the direction which I have already indicated. By these details I mean freedom of the press, the rights of forming societies, freedom of religion, election of representatives of the people, and many other rights, which will have to vanish from the daily life of man. If they do not altogether vanish, they will have to be fundamentally changed the day after the announcement of the new constitution. It would only be at this particular moment that it would be quite safe for us to announce all our changes, and for the following reason: all perceptible changes at any other time might prove dangerous, because, if they were forcibly introduced and strictly and indiscriminately enforced, they might exasperate the people, as these would fear fresh changes in similar

Protocol # 5 -

THE TOTALITARIAN STATE

Protocols will take every right and freedom you have away from you. This is not the Jewish way of governing.

The *Protocols* was translated into English as The Jewish Peril in 1920. In fact, the original *Protocols* in this book were taken from that very first English translation.

directions. On the other hand, if the changes were to entail yet more indulgences, people would say that we recognise our mistakes and that, might detract from the glory of infallibility of the new power. They might also say that we had been frightened and were forced to yield. And were this the case, the world would never thank us, as they regard it as a right always to have concessions made to them. If either of these impressions were made on the mind of the public, it would be extremely dangerous for the prestige of the new constitution.

It is essential for us that, from the first moment of its proclamation, whilst the people will be still suffering from the effects of the sudden change and will be in a state of terror and indecision, that they should realise that we are so powerful, so invulnerable, and so full of might, that we shall in no case take their interests into consideration. We shall want them to understand that we will not only ignore their opinion and wishes, but will be ready at any moment or place to suppress with a strong hand any expression or hint of opposition. We shall want the people to understand that we have taken everything we wanted and that we will not, under any circumstances, allow them to share our power. Then they will close their eyes to everything out of fear and will patiently await further developments.

The Gentiles are like a flock of sheep—we are the wolves. And do you not know what the sheep do when wolves penetrate in to the sheepfold? They close their eyes to everything. To this they will be also driven, because we will promise to return to them all their liberties after subduing the world's enemies and after bringing all parties into subjection. I need hardly tell you how long they would have to wait for the return of their liberties.

Protocols require a totalitarian state.

Where have we read that before? Like sheep being taken to the slaughter. This is not the abundant life that God has promised His children!

Henry Ford, the automobile industrialist, originally supported the *Protocols*. A Russian royalist convinced Ford to publish the *Protocols* in the United States of America. Ford owned the Dearborn Independent newspaper, which is where the *Protocols* was first published in the United States. Between May and September, 1920, a 250-page paperback collection of anti-Semitic articles were published in a series called "The International Jew: the World's Foremost Problem." It sold for 25 cents. Then Ford published it in a book which was translated into 16 languages and printed by the millions. It was called The International Jew.

For what reason were we induced to invent our policy and to instill the same into the Gentiles? We instilled this policy into them without letting them understand its inner meaning. What prompted us to adopt such a line of action, if it was not because we could not, as a scattered race, attain our object by direct means, but only by circumvention? This was the real cause and origin of our organisation of masonry, which those swine of Gentiles do not fathom, and the aims of which they do not even suspect. They are decoyed by us into our mass of lodges, which appear to be nothing more than masonic in order to throw dust in the eyes of their comrades.

By the mercy of God His chosen people were scattered, and in this dispersal, which seemed to the world to be our weakness, has proved to be all our power, which has now brought us to the threshold of universal sovereignty.

We have not much more to build on these foundations in order to attain our aims.

* * * * *

The word liberty, which can be interpreted in divers ways, we will define thus :—" Liberty is the right of doing what is permitted by law." Such a definition of this word will be useful to us in this way, that it will rest with us to say where there shall be liberty and where there may not, and for the simple reason that law will permit only what is desirable to us.

With the Press we will deal in the following manner :— What is the part played by the Press at the present time? It serves to rouse in the people furious passions or sometimes egoistic party disputes, which may be necessary for our purpose. It is often empty, unjust, false, and most people do not in the least understand its exact purposes. We will harness it and will guide it with firm reins, we will

Several evangelicals are now against the Masons because they say they disobey scripture by "taking a secret oath?"

Protocol # 12 - CONTROL OF THE PRESS

Dictatorships can only survive if they CONTROL the press!

I must admit it is ironic that the *Protocols* in America was introduced in Dearborn, Michigan. Modern-day Dearborn is today, one of the most populated conclaves of Muslims in America. Strange coincidence? **I think not!**

also have to gain control of all other publishing firms. It would be of no use for us to control the newspaper press, if we were still to remain exposed to the attacks of pamphlets and books. We will turn the, at present, expensive production of publication into a profitable resource to our government by introducing a special stamp duty, and by forcing publishers and typographers to pay us a deposit, in order to guarantee our government from any kind of assaults on the part of the press. In case of an attack, we will impose fines right and left. Such measures as stamps, deposits, and fines will be a large source of income to the government. Certainly party papers would not mind paying heavy fines, but, after a second serious attack on us, we would suppress them altogether. No one will be able with impunity to touch the prestige of our political infallibility. For closing down publications we will give the following pretext :—The publication, which is being suppressed excites, we will say, public opinion without any ground or foundation. But I would ask you to bear in mind that amongst the aggressive publications will be those which have been instituted by us for this purpose. But they will only attack such points in our policy as we intend changing. No piece of information will reach society without passing through our control. This we are attaining even at the present time by the fact that all news is received by a few agencies, in which it is centralised from all parts of the world. When we attain power these agencies will belong to us entirely and will only publish such news as we choose to allow.

If under the present conditions we have managed to gain control of the Gentile society to such an extent that it surveys the world's affairs through the coloured glasses which we put over its eyes; if even now there exists no

Centralized news control will control the masses!

Look at every coup, and you will see that the totalitarian head has gone to the news center first.

The *Protocols* in America was widely successful due to the "Red Scare" and the abhorrence of the persecution of Christians by the Communists. The fact that religious Jews were just as much persecuted was never revealed or believed at the time. The "thought patterns" of America were "ripe" for a belief that a Jewish world government could possibly exist. Many even believed that Jews were behind communism and socialism.

impediment to hinder our access to state secrets, as they are called by the stupidity of the Gentiles, what will be our position, when we shall be officially recognised as rulers of the world, in the person of our world-governing Emperor?

Let us return to the future of the press. Anybody desiring to become an editor, librarian, or printer, will be compelled to obtain a certificate and licence, which, in case of disobedience, would be withdrawn. The canals, through which human thought finds its expression, will by these means be delivered into the hands of our government, which will use the same as an educational organ, and will thus prevent the public from being drawn astray by idealising "progress" and liberalism. Who of us does not know that this fantastic blessing is a straight road to utopia, from which have sprung anarchy and hatred towards authority? This is for the simple reason that "progress," or rather the idea of liberal progress, gave the people different ideas of emancipation, without setting any limit to it. All so-called liberals are anarchists, if not in their action, certainly by ideas. Each one of them runs after the phantom of liberty, thinking that he can do whatever he wishes, that is to say, falling into a state of anarchy in the opposition which he offers for the mere sake of opposition.

Let us now discuss the press. We will tax it in the same manner as the newspaper press—that is to say, by means of excise stamps and deposits. But on books of less than 300 pages we will place a tax twice as heavy. These short books we will classify as pamphlets in order to diminish the publication of periodicals, which constitute the most virulent form of printed poison. These measures will also compel writers to publish such long works that they will be little read by the public, and chiefly so on

A "world-governing Emperor" has no resemblance to any Jewish law!

THIS IS AN OUTRIGHT FRAUD!

As a direct result of the *Protocols*, many Americans believed that the Jews caused World War One, and that the Jews betrayed the United States. It didn't matter that in Germany 100,000 Jews participated in World War One and that 78,000 served time at the front; it was "irrelevant" that 12,000 Jews lost their lives in battle, and that 30,000 received medals for bravery!

account of their high price. We ourselves will publish cheap works in order to educate and set the mind of the public in the direction that we desire. Taxation will bring about a reduction in the writing of aimless leisure literature, and the fact that they are responsible before the law will place authors in our hands. No one desirous of attacking us with his pen would find a publisher.

Before printing any kind of work, the publisher or printer will have to apply to the authorities for a permit to publish the said work. Thus we shall know beforehand of any conspiracy against us, and we shall be able to knock it on the head by anticipating the plot and publishing an explanation.

The Protocols is a "Weapon of Mass Deception!"

Literature and journalism are the two most important educational powers; for this reason our government will buy up the greater number of periodicals. By these means we shall neutralise the bad influence of the private press and obtain an enormous influence over the human mind. If we were to allow ten private periodicals we should ourselves start thirty, and so forth.

But the public must not have the slightest suspicion of these measures, therefore all periodicals published by us will seem to be of contradictory views and opinions, thus inspiring confidence and presenting an attractive appearance to our unsuspecting enemies, who will thus fall into our trap and will be disarmed.

In the front row we will place the official press. It will always be on guard in defence of our interests and therefore its influence on the public will be comparatively insignificant. In the second row we will place the semi-official press, the duty of which will be to attract the indifferent and lukewarm. In the third row we will place what will purport to be our opposition, which in one of

In short, people believed the lie for so long—the lie became "the truth."

In reality, Henry Ford recanted the *Protocols* in 1926 when he was threatened with a libel suit.

its publications will appear to be our adversary. Our real enemies will take this opposition into their confidence and will let us see their cards.

All our newspapers will support different parties—aristocratic, republican, revolutionary, and even anarchical—but, of course, only so long as constitutions last. These newspapers, like the Indian god Vishnu, will be possessed of hundreds of hands, each of which will be feeling the pulse of varying public opinion.

When the pulse becomes quick, these hands will incline this opinion towards our cause, because a nervous subject is easily led and easily falls under any kind of influence.

If any chatterers are going to imagine that they are repeating the opinion of their party newspaper, they will in reality be repeating our own opinion, or the opinion which we desire. Thinking that they are following the organ of this party, they will in reality be following the flag which we will fly for them. In order that our newspaper army may carry out the spirit of this programme of appearing to support various parties, we must organise our press with great care.

Under the name of Central Commission of the Press, we will organise literary meetings, at which our agents unnoticed will give the countersign and the passwords. By discussing and contradicting our policy, of course always superficially, without really touching on the important parts of it, our organs will carry on feigned debates with official newspapers in order to give us an excuse for defining our plans with more accuracy than we could do in our preliminary announcements. But this, of course, only when it is to our advantage. This opposition on the part of the press will also serve the purpose of making the people believe that liberty of speech still exists. To

The Protocols is a perfect example of the principle that if you tell a lie often enough, not matter how blatant and ridiculous, it will begin to be accepted as truth.

This is an entire deception of the truth and a deception of reality.

Ford said: "...To my great regret I learn that in the '<u>Dearborn Independent</u>' there appeared articles which induced the Jews to regard me as their enemy promoting anti-Semitism? I am mortified that this Journal...is giving currency to '*The Protocols of the Wise Men of Zion,*' which I learn to be gross forgeries. I deem it my duty...to make amends for the wrong done to the Jews as fellow men and brothers by asking their forgiveness..."

our agents it will give an opportunity of showing that our opponents bring senseless accusations against us, being unable to find a real ground on which to refute our policy.

Such measures, which will escape the notice of public attention, will be the most successful means of guiding the public mind and of inspiring confidence in favour of our government.

Thanks to these measures, we will be able to excite or calm the public mind on political questions, when it becomes necessary for us to do so; we will be able to persuade or confuse them by printing true or false news, facts or contradictions, according as it will suit our purpose. The information which we will publish will depend on the manner in which the people are at the time accepting that kind of news, and we will always take great care to feel the ground before treading on it.

The restrictions which, as I have said, we will impose on private publications, will enable us to make a certainty of defeating our enemies, because they will not have press organs at their disposal by means of which they could truly give full vent to their opinions. We shall not even have to make a thorough refutation of their statements.

Ballons d'essai, which we will throw into the third row of our press, we will, if necessary, semi-officially refute.

Already there exists in French journalism a system of masonic understanding for giving countersigns. All organs of the press are tied by mutual professional secrets in the manner of the ancient oracles. Not one of its members will betray his knowledge of the secret, if such a secret has not been ordered to be made public. No single publisher will have the courage to betray the secret entrusted to him, the reason being that not one of them is admitted into the literary world without bearing the

Controlling information is important. In fact, Sergei Nilus gave his first copy of the Protocols to the Russian Czar!

Along with the Jews, the Freemasons were blamed for the 1905 Russian Revolution.

The *Protocols* portrays the Jews and Freemasons as strangers and adversaries of Christian civilization. It highlights their apparently odd and outlandish rituals, their supposedly secret symbols and secret contacts, their influence, their control over media, and their exploitation of the most diverse political parties.

marks of some shady act in his past life. He would only have to show the least sign of disobedience and the mark would be immediately revealed. Whilst these marks remain known only to a few, the prestige of the journalist attracts public opinion throughout the country. The people follow and admire him.

Our plans must extend chiefly to the provinces. It is essential for us to create such ideas and inspire such opinions there as we could at any time launch on the capital by producing them as the neutral views of the provinces.

Of course, the source and origin of the idea would not be altered: namely, it would be ours.

It is imperative for us that, before we assume power, cities should sometimes be under the influence of the opinion of the provinces—that is to say, that they should know the opinion of the majority, which will have been prearranged by us. It is necessary for us that the capitals, at the critical psychological moment, should not have time to discuss an accomplished fact, but should accept it simply because it has been passed by a majority in the provinces.

Instead of listening to the majority, you need to do what Proverbs 1:33 says: "Whoever listens to me will dwell safely, and will be secure, without fear of evil."

When we reach the period of the new *régime*—that is to say, during the transition stage to our sovereignty—we must not allow the press to publish any account of criminal cases; it will be essential that people should think that the new *régime* is so satisfactory that even crime has ceased.

Where criminal cases occur, they must remain known only to their victim and any one who may have chanced to witness them, and to those alone.

* * * * *

Protocol # 13 - Deals with Distractions

The need of daily bread will force the Gentiles to hold their tongues and to remain our humble servants. Those

To many, the Jews and Freemasons are one and the same; which, of course, is not true.

Freemasons made the advocates of the *Protocols* feel very uneasy.

of the Gentiles whom we may be employing in our press will, under orders from us, discuss facts to which it would not be desirable that we should especially refer in our official gazette. And, whilst all manner of discussions and disputes are thus taking place, we will pass the laws which we need and will place them before the public as an accomplished fact.

No one will dare to demand that what has been decided on should be repealed, more especially as we will make it appear as if it were our intention to help progress. Then the press will draw the attention of the public away by new propositions (you know for yourselves that we have always taught the populace to seek new emotions). Brainless political adventurers will hasten to discuss the new problems, such people who even nowadays do not understand what they are talking about. Political problems are not meant to be understood by ordinary people; they can only be comprehended, as I have said before, by rulers who have been directing affairs for many centuries. From all this you may conclude that, when we shall defer to public opinion, we shall do so in order to ease the working of our machinery. You can also perceive that we seek approval for the various questions not by deeds, but by words. We continually assert that, in all our measures, we are guided by the hope and certainty of serving the common welfare.

In order to distract overrestless people from discussing political questions, we provide them with new problems—that is to say, those of trade and commerce. Over such questions let them become as excited as they like! The masses consent to abstain and desist from what they think is political activity only if we can give them some new amusements, that is to say, commerce, which we try

The Protocols suggests a pre-arranged set of laws, without the people's consent. Many times Americans are angered when a president goes around Congress; or when Congressmen "go around" the law.

MINDLESS politicians are NOT the Judeo form of governance.

The term "Freemasons" was birthed in England in the eleventh century. These workers did not belong to any particular local "guild" of bricklayers, for instance. They would travel from city to city plying their particular trade. They were organized into what they called "lodges." These log houses were originally used as work stations or meeting rooms. Freemasons were a secretive and private group and so that gave rise to all kinds of speculation. They were continually under threat of suppression from the organized church and irreligious authorities. Since they were such an independent group of thinkers, many had conspiratorial ideas and plans.

and make them believe is also a political question. We ourselves induced the masses to take part in politics in order to secure their support in our campaign against the Gentile governments.

In order to keep them from discovering for themselves any new line of action in politics, we will also distract them by various kinds of amusements, games, pastimes, passions, public houses, and so on.

Soon we shall start advertising in the press, inviting people to enter for various competitions in all manner of enterprises, such as art, sport, etc. These new interests will definitely distract the public mind from such questions which we would have to contest with the populace. As the people will gradually lose the gift of thinking for themselves, they will shout together with us, for the sole reason that we shall be the only members of society who will be in a position to advance new lines of thought, which lines we will advance by means of using as our tools only such persons as could not be suspected of being allied with us. The part of liberal idealists will be definitely terminated when our government is recognised. Until then they will do us good service. For this reason we will try to direct the public mind towards every kind of fantastic theory which could appear progressive or liberal. It was we who, with complete success, turned the brainless heads of the Gentiles by our theories of progress towards socialism; there is not to be found a brain among the Gentiles which would perceive that in every instance, behind the word "progress" is hidden a deviation from the truth, except in such cases where this word refers to material of scientific discoveries. For there is but one true teaching, and in it there is no room for "progress." Progress, like a false idea, serves to conceal the truth in

Protocols require more distractions from government—to keep them in power!

The Bible says to set your face like a flint to the front—not to look to the right, or to the left! NO DISTRACTIONS.

Most people believed the Freemasons to be involved in a secret war against the monarchy and against the Pope. This tightly-knit group was organized in a very strict order of hierarchy, ultimately answering to the Grand Master.

Jews had nothing to do with the composition of the Masonic rituals. The real explanation of the Hebrew elements in Freemasonry, as in Templarism, is that both borrowed from the Old Testament, as a Christian document.

That's right; the Jews ARE "God's Chosen People!" Now, that was a truthful statement!

Protocol # 14 - an ALL-OUT ASSAULT upon religion.

Establishment of a One World Religion is outlined in the deceitful Protocols.

order that nobody should know truth besides ourselves, God's Chosen People, whom he has elected as its guardian.

When we get into power, our orators will discuss the great problems which have been convulsing humanity in order, in the end, to bring mankind under our blessed rule.

Who will, then, suspect that all these problems were instigated by us in accordance with a political scheme which has been understood by no man for so many centuries?

*** * * * ***

When we establish ourselves as lords of the earth, we will not tolerate any other religion except that of our own, namely, a religion recognising God alone, with whom our fate is bound by His election of us and by Whom also the fate of the world is determined.

For this reason we must destroy all professions of faith. If the temporary result of this is to produce atheists, it will not interfere with our object, but will act as an example to those generations to come, who will listen to our teaching on the religion of Moses which, by its resolute and well-considered doctrine, committed to us the duty of subduing all nations under our feet.

By doing this we shall also lay stress on the mystic truths of the Mosaic teachings on which, we shall say, is based all its educative power.

Then, on every possible occasion we will publish articles, in which we will compare our beneficial rule with that of the past. The state of blessedness and peace which will then exist, in spite of its having been brought about by centuries of disturbance, will also serve to illustrate the benevolence of our new rule. The mistakes made by the Gentiles in their administration will be demonstrated

After World War One, religious anti-Semitism was very much alive and well. In fact, in France, it greatly flourished. More than 30 editions of the *Protocols* were written with numerous commentaries. The hatred documents helped the Fascists in Italy and General Franco in Spain. The *Protocols* even expanded the fear of Stalin. Globally, the *Protocols* continued to be printed and published at an alarming rate, in spite of it being judged a "fraud" by most.

by us in the most vivid colours. We will start such a feeling of disgust towards the former *régime* that the nations will prefer a state of peace in a condition of enslavement, to the rights of the much-lauded liberty, which has so cruelly tortured them and drained from them the very source of human existence, and to which they were really only instigated by a crowd of adventurers who knew not what they did.

Useless changes of government, to which we have been prompting the Gentiles and by this means undermining their state edifice, will by that time have so worried the nations that they will prefer to endure anything from us out of fear of having to return to the turmoils and misfortunes which they will have gone through. We will draw special attention to the historical mistakes of the Gentile Governments, by which they tormented humanity for so many centuries in their lack of understanding anything that regards true welfare of human life and in their search for fantastic plans of social welfare. For the Gentiles have not noticed that their plans, instead of improving the relations of man to man, have only made them worse and worse. And these relations are the very foundations of human existence. The whole force of our principles and measures will be in the fact that they will be explained by us as being in bright contrast to the broken-down *régime* of former social conditions.

Our philosophers will expose all the disadvantages of Gentile religions, but no one will ever judge our religion from its true point of view, because nobody will ever have a thorough knowledge of it except our own people, who will never venture to unveil its mysteries.

In the so-considered leading countries, we have circulated an insane, dirty and disgusting literature. For a

D

We are in a constant daily battle—the battle for your mind! It is always good versus evil. You have choices to make every moment!

The Protocols wants to use the Jews to blame the Gentiles for all the world's problems.

The *Protocols* quickly began to circulate around the world. A German edition appeared in 1919. Many European countries embraced the *Protocols* between the two world wars. Russian exiles in Siberia brought the *Protocols* to Japan where it was published in Japanese in 1924.

short time after the recognition of our rule, we shall continue to encourage the prevalence of such a literature, in order that it should the more pointedly mark the contrast of the teachings which we will issue from our exalted position. Our learned men, who were educated for the purpose of leading the Gentiles, will make speeches, draw up plans, sketch notes and write articles, by means of which we will influence men's minds, inclining them towards that knowledge and those ideas which will suit us.

Protocol # 15 - RUTHLESS SUPPRESSION

When we shall eventually have obtained power by means of a number of *coups d'état* which will be arranged by us, so that they should take place simultaneously in all countries, and immediately after their respective governments shall have been officially pronounced as incapable of ruling the populace--a considerable period of time may elapse before this is realised, perhaps a whole century—we will make every endeavour to prevent conspiracies being made against us. In order to attain this end we will make merciless use of executions with regard to all who may take up arms against the establishment of our power.

Any government or doctrine that promotes senseless executions or murders is not of God.

The institutions of any fresh secret society will be also punishable by death; but those secret societies which exist at the present time and which are known to us, which are serving and have served our purpose, we will dismiss and exile their members to remote parts of the world. Such is the manner in which we will deal with any Gentile Freemasons who may know more than will suit our convenience. Such masons whom we may for some reason or other pardon, we shall keep in continual fear of being sent into exile. We will pass a law which will condemn all former members of secret societies to be

The *Protocols* served as a genuine "catalyst" in drawing a line in the sand between fascists and antifascists. The political consequences of the *Protocols* were enormous.

Robert Wilton of the London Times and Victor Marsden of the Morning Post, two British correspondents, each of whom had lived in pre-Communist Russia, promoted the idea of Jewish conspiracy in Great Britain. Eighteen articles on the subject of a Jewish conspiracy as well as the *Protocols* itself were published in the Morning Post in the 1920's.

exiled from Europe, where we shall have the centre of our government.

The decisions of our Government will be final, and no one will have the right of appeal.

In order to call to heel all Gentile societies, in which we have so deeply implanted dissensions and the tenets of the protestant religion, merciless measures will have to be introduced. Such measures should show the nations that our power cannot be infringed. We must take no account of the numerous victims who will have to be sacrificed in order to obtain future prosperity.

To attain prosperity even by means of numerous sacrifices is the duty of a government, which realises that the conditions of its existence do not only lie in the privileges which it enjoys, but also in the executions of its duty.

The main condition of its stability lies in the strengthening of the prestige of its power, and this prestige can only be obtained by majestic and unshakable might, which should show that it is inviolable and surrounded by a mystic power; for example, that it is by God appointed.

Such has been, up to the present time, the Russian Autocracy, our only dangerous enemy, if we are not to include the Holy See. Remember, at the time when Italy was streaming with blood, she did not touch a hair of Silla's head, and he was the man who made her blood pour out. Owing to his strength of character, Silla became a god in the eyes of the populace, and his fearless return to Italy made him inviolable. The populace will not harm the man who hypnotises it by his courage and strength of mind.

Until the time when we attain power we will try to create and multiply lodges of freemasons in all parts

Jews forgave their enemies who would try to bring them harm. "Even as Christ forgave you, so you also must do!"

– Colossians 3:13

Marsden translated the *Protocols* into English and in his introduction to the document commented: "The Jews are carrying it out with steadfast purpose, creating wars and revolutions...to destroy the white Gentile race, that the Jews may seize the power during the resulting chaos and rule with their claimed superior intelligence over the remaining races of the world, as kings over slaves."

Using Masonic lodges as "propaganda centers." This is not the Jewish way; nor God's way.

of the world. We will entice into these lodges all, who may become, or who are known to be public-spirited. These lodges will be the main place from which we shall obtain our information, as well as being propaganda centres.

We will centralise all these lodges under one management, known to us alone, and which will consist of our learned men. These lodges will also have their own representatives, in order to screen where the management really lies. And this management will alone have the right of deciding who may speak, and of drawing up the order of the day. In these lodges we will tie the knot of all socialistic and revolutionary classes of society. The most secret political plans will be known to us and will be guided by us in their execution as soon as they are formed.

Nearly all the agents in the international and secret police will be members of our lodges.

The services of the police are of extreme importance to us, as they are able to throw a screen over our enterprises, invent reasonable explanations for discontent among the masses, as well as punish those who refuse to submit.

Most people who enter secret societies are adventurers, who want somehow to make their way in life, and who are not seriously minded.

With such people it will be easy for us to pursue our object, and we will make them set our machinery in motion.

If the whole world becomes perturbed, it will only signify that it was necessary for us to so perturb it in order to destroy its too great solidity. If conspiracies start in the midst of it, this will mean that one of our most

Despite the miraculous growth and success of *Protocols* worldwide, there was widespread official condemnation of the fraud.

For example, the Swiss Jewish community launched an official judicial attack against the *Protocols* with a trial that began in 1933. During that trial, the distinguished plaintiffs made very clear that the *Protocols* had been fabricated. It came to light that the Russian Secret Police helped in the obvious plagiarism.

Judge Walter Meyer found in favor of the plaintiffs on May 14, 1935. He stated that the *Protocols* was, in fact, a forgery and a work of plagiarism.

faithful agents is at the head of the said conspiracy. It is only natural that we should be the sole people who direct masonic enterprises. We are the only people who know how to direct them. We know the final aim of each action, whereas the Gentiles are ignorant of most things concerning masonry, they cannot even see the immediate results of what they are doing. They generally think only of the immediate advantages of the moment, and are content if their pride is satisfied in the fulfilment of their intention, and do not perceive that the original idea was not their own, but was inspired by ourselves.

The Gentiles frequent Masonic Lodges out of pure curiosity, or in the hope of receiving their share of the good things which are going, and some of them do so in order to be able to discuss their own idiotic ideas before an audience. The Gentiles are on the look-out for the emotions of success and applause; these are distributed freely by us. That is why we let them have their success, in order to turn to our advantage the men possessed by feelings of self-pride, who, without noticing it, absorb our ideas, confident in the conviction of their own infallibility, and that they alone have ideas and are not subject to the influence of others.

You have no idea how easy it is to bring even the most clever of the Gentiles to a ridiculous state of *naïveté* by working on his conceit, and, on the other hand, how easy it is to discourage him by the smallest failure or even by simply ceasing to applaud him and thus bring him to a state of servile subjection, holding out to him the prospect of some new success. Just as our people despise success, and are only anxious to see their plans realised, so the Gentiles love success and are prepared to sacrifice all their plans for its sake. This feature in the character of

The Bible tells us to "not be heady or high-minded."

No conceit! God wants us to walk humble before all men!

The Judge wrote:

"I hope that one day there will come a time when no one will any longer comprehend how in the year 1935 almost a dozen fully sensible and reasonable men could for fourteen days torment their brains before a court of Berne over the authenticity or lack of authenticity of these so-called *Protocols*...that, for all the harm they have already caused and may yet cause, are nothing but ridiculous nonsense."

the Gentiles renders it much easier for us to do what we like with them. Those who appear to be tigers are as stupid as sheep, and their heads are full of emptiness.

We will let them ride in their dreams on the horse of idle hopes of destroying human individuality by symbolic ideas of collectivism. They have not yet understood, and never will understand, that this wild dream is contrary to the principal law of nature, which, from the very beginning of the world, created a being unlike all others in order that he should have individuality.

Does not the fact that we were capable of bringing the Gentiles to such an erroneous idea prove, with striking clearness, what a narrow conception they have of human life in comparison with ourselves? Herein lies the greatest hope of our success. How farseeing were our wise men of old when they told us that, in order to attain a really great object we must not stop short before the means, nor count the number of victims who must be sacrificed for the achievement of the cause! We never counted the victims of the seed of those brutes of Gentiles, and, although we have sacrificed many of our own people, we have already given them such a position in this world as they formerly never dreamt that they would attain. Comparatively few victims on our side have safeguarded our nation from destruction. Every man must inevitably end by death. It is better to hasten this end in the case of people who impede our cause than in that of those who advance it. We put freemasons to death in such a manner that no one, except the brotherhood, can have the least suspicion of the fact; not even the victims themselves suspect beforehand. They all die, when it is necessary, apparently from a natural death. Knowing these facts, even the brotherhood itself dares not protest against it.

GOD HATES ARROGANCE!

YES, it is appointed unto man "once to die." But then— "after that, the judgment!"

Three additional trials rendered judgment against the validity of the *Protocols*:

In Johannesburg, South Africa in 1991.

In Prague, Czechoslovakia in 1993

In Moscow, Russia in 1993

By such means we have cut to the very root of protest against our orders so far as the freemasons themselves are concerned. We preach liberalism to the Gentiles, but on the other hand we keep our own nation in entire subjection.

Under our influence the laws of the Gentiles have been obeyed as little as possible. The prestige of their laws has been undermined by liberal ideas, which have been introduced by us into their midst. The most important questions, both political and moral, are decided by the Courts of Justice in whatever manner we prescribe. The Gentile administrator of justice looks upon cases in whatever light we choose to expose them. This we accomplished by means of our agents and people with whom we appear to have no connection: opinions of the press and other means; even senators and other high officials blindly follow our advice.

The brain of the Gentile, being of a purely bestial character, is incapable of analysing and observing anything and moreover of foreseeing to what the development of a case may lead if it is placed in a certain light.

It is just in this difference of mentality between the Gentiles and ourselves that we can easily see the mark of our election by God and superhuman nature, when it is compared with the instinctive bestial brain of the Gentiles. They only see facts, but do not foresee them, and are incapable of inventing anything, with the exception, perhaps, only of things material. From all this it is clear that nature herself meant us to lead and rule the world. When the time comes for us to govern openly, the moment will come to show the benevolence of our rule, and we shall amend all the laws. Our laws will be short, clear and concise, requiring no interpretation, so that everybody

A totalitarian state is NOT a free, Jewish state!

"For God has not given us a spirit of fear, but of power and of love and of a sound mind."

– 2 Timothy 1:7

In 1964, a United States Congressional investigation issued a report on the "*Protocols of Zion.*" The Judiciary Committee in its introductory statement said:

"Every age and country has had its share of fabricated 'historic' documents which have been foisted on an unsuspecting public for some malign purpose. In the United States such forgeries crop up periodically in the underworld of sub-politics. One of the most notorious and most durable of these is the Protocols of the Elders of Zion."

will be able to know them inside out. The main feature in them will be the obedience required towards authority, and this respect for authority will be carried to a very high pitch. Then all kinds of abuse of power will cease, because everybody will be responsible before the one supreme power, namely that of the sovereign. The abuse of power on the part of people other than the sovereign will be so severely punished that all will lose the desire to try their strength in this respect.

We shall closely watch each step taken by our administrative body, from which will depend the working of the state machine; because, if the administration becomes slack, disorder will arise everywhere. Not a single illegal act or abuse of power will remain unpunished.

Strict judicial judgments are not judicious at all in a totalitarian state.

All acts of concealment and of wilful neglect on the part of officials of the administration will disappear after they have seen the first examples of punishment.

The grandness of our might will require that suitable punishments should be awarded, that is to say, that they should be harsh, even in the case of the smallest attempt to violate the prestige of our authority for the sake of personal gain. The man who suffers for his faults, even if too severely, will be like a soldier dying on the battlefield of the administration in the cause of power, principle, and law, which admit of no deviation from the public path for the sake of personal interests, even in the case of those who drive the public chariot. For example, our judges will know that, by attempting to show their indulgence, they will violate the law of justice, which is made in order to award an exemplary punishment to men for the offences which they have committed, and not in order to enable the judge to show his clemency. This good quality ought only to be shown in private life, and not in the official

"He has shown you, O man, what is good; and what does the Lord require of you but to do justly, to love mercy, and to walk humbly with your God?" - Micah 6:8 This is God's version of "clemency."

"The undersigned Senators have, therefore, recommended the publication of the following analysis by the subcommittee in order to lay to rest any honest question concerning the nature, origin, and significance of this ancient canard.

"Essentially, this study is a compendium of a number of separate analyses by authorities in several countries who have had occasion to investigate the origins and circulation of the Protocols." (Signed by United States Senators Thomas J. Dodd and Kenneth B. Keating)

capacity of a judge, which influences the whole basis of the education of mankind.

Members of the law will not serve in the courts after 55 years of age for the following reasons :—

1. Because old men adhere more firmly to preconceived ideas and are less capable of obeying new orders.

2. Because such a measure will enable us to make frequent changes in the staff, which will thus be subject to any pressure on our part. Any man who wishes to retain his post will, in order to secure this, have to obey us blindly. In general our judges will be selected from among men who understand that their duty is to punish and to apply laws, and not to indulge in dreams of liberalism, which might injure the educational scheme of the government, as the Gentile judges at present do. Our scheme for changing officials will also help us to destroy any kind of combination which they might form among themselves, and so they will work solely in the interest of the government, from which their fate will depend. The rising generation of judges will be so educated that they will instinctively prevent any action which might harm the existing relations of our subjects one to another.

At present judges of the Gentiles are indulgent to all manner of criminals, for they do not possess the correct idea of their duty, and for the simple reason that rulers, when appointing judges, do not impress the idea of their duty upon them.

The rulers of the Gentiles, when nominating their subjects to important posts, do not trouble to explain to them the importance of the same and for what purpose the posts in question were created; they act like animals when these send their young out in search of prey. Thus the governments of the Gentiles fall to pieces at the

Protocols can only work through MIND CONTROL!

True justice and mercy is the God that the Jews serve!

The *Protocols* is one of many fraudulent documents that advocate the myth of an "international Jewish conspiracy." In recent years, for example, documents that are strikingly similar to the *Protocols* have been printed in the Soviet Union as part of the persistent campaign against the Jewish minority there. The one difference is that the documents circulated in the Soviet Union tend to equate "international Jewry" with "international capitalism."

hands of their own administrators. We will take one more moral, drawn from the results of the system adopted by the Gentiles, and use it for the edification of our government.

We will root out all liberal tendencies from every important institution of propaganda in our government, from which may depend the education of all those who will be our subjects. These important posts will be reserved exclusively for those who were specially educated by us for administration.

Should it be observed that to put our officials prematurely on the retired list might prove too expensive for our government, I will reply that, first of all, we shall try to find private occupation for such officials in order to compensate them for the loss of their posts in government employment, or else that, in any case, our government will be in possession of all the money in the world, therefore expense will not come into consideration.

Our autocracy will be consistent in all its actions, therefore any decision which our high command may choose to take will always be treated with respect and unconditionally obeyed. We shall ignore any kind of grumbling or dissatisfaction, and punish every sign of discontent so severely that other people will accept it as an example for themselves.

We will cancel the right of appeal and reserve it only for our own use; the reason being that we must not allow the idea to grow up among the people that our judges are capable of erring in their decisions.

In case of a judgment requiring revision, we will immediately depose the judge in question and publicly punish him, in order that such an error should not occur again.

This fraud advises that they will control ALL of the money in the world. YES, a "One World Bank"—the ultimate in control over people.

Jews have a very special way for their people to appeal a judge's decision; but "NO APPEAL" IS NOT IT!

Many notable authorities have agreed that the *Protocols* are fraudulent: For instance:

Hugo Valentin, lecturer in history at the University of Upsala in Sweden, characterized the *Protocols* in his 1936 study Anti-Semitism, Historically and Critically Examined as "THE GREATEST FORGERY OF THE CENTURY."

I repeat what I have said before, namely that one of our main principles will be to watch administrative officials, and this chiefly in order to satisfy the nation, because it has a full right to insist that a good government should have good administrative officials.

Our government will bear the appearance of a patriarchal trust in the person of our ruler. Our nation and our subjects will look upon him as upon a father, who takes care to satisfy all their needs, looks after all their actions and arranges the dealings of his subjects one with another, as well as their dealings with the government. Thus the feeling of reverence towards the ruler will penetrate so deeply into the nation that it will not be able to exist without his care and leadership. They cannot live in peace without him, and will finally recognise him as their sovereign autocrat.

Many times, anti-Semitism is used as a smokescreen for one's own EVIL DESIGNS!

The people will have such a deep feeling of reverence towards him as will approach adoration, especially when they are convinced that his officials blindly execute his order and that he alone rules over them. They will rejoice to see us regulate our lives as if we were parents desirous of educating their children with a keen sense of duty and obedience.

As regards our secret policy, all nations are children, and their governments also. As you can see for yourselves, I base our despotism on Right and on Duty. The right of the government to insist that people should do their duty is in itself an obligation of the ruler, who is the father of his subjects. Right of might is granted to him in order that he should lead humanity in the direction laid down by the laws of nature, that is to say towards obedience.

Every creature in this world is under subjection, if not under that of a man, then under that of circumstances

Father Pierre Charles, Professor of Theology at the Jesuit College in Louvain, France, stated in a 1938 essay: "It has been proved that these *Protocols* are a fraud, a clumsy plagiarism...made for the purpose of rendering Jews odious..."

In 1942, several prominent historians, including Carl Becker of Cornell, Sydney Fay and William Langer of Harvard, and Allan Nevins and Carlton J. H. Hayes of Columbia, introduced Professor John Shelton Curtiss' '<u>An Appraisal of the Protocols of Zion</u>' with their endorsements of his findings as "completely destructive of the historicity of the *Protocols* and as establishing beyond doubt the fact that they are rank and pernicious forgeries."

Our Bible says, Beware: when people shall say peace and safety! You must always be on your guard for those arrogant people who will try to fool you with a false peace.

Protocol # 16 - BRAINWASHING... and it starts with our children and the educational system to control them already in place in our schools!

or under that of its own nature, in any case under something that is more powerful than itself. Therefore let us be more powerful for the sake of the common cause.

We must, without hesitation, sacrifice such individuals as may have violated the existing order, because in exemplary punishment is the solution of the great educational problem.

On the day when the King of Israel places upon his sacred head the crown, presented to him by the whole of Europe, he will become the Patriarch of the world.

The number of victims, who will have to be sacrificed by our King, will never exceed the number of those who have been sacrificed by Gentile sovereigns in their quest for greatness and in their rivalry with one another.

Our sovereign will be in constant communication with the people, he will deliver speeches from tribunes, which speeches will be immediately circulated all over the world.

* * * * *

With the object of destroying any kind of collective enterprise, other than our own, we will annihilate collective work in its initial stage—that is to say, we will transform the universities and reconstruct them according to our own plans.

The heads of the universities and their professors will be specially prepared by means of elaborate secret programmes of action, in which they will be instructed and from which they will not be able to deviate with impunity. They will be very carefully nominated and will be entirely dependent on the Government. We will exclude from our syllabus all teachings of civil law, as well as of any other political subject. Only a few men from among the initiated will be selected for their conspicuous abilities, in order to be taught these sciences. Universities will

In 1961, Richard Helms, then Assistant Director of the CIA, stated at a Senate subcommittee hearing: "The Russians have a long tradition in the art of forgery. More than 60 years ago the Czarist intelligence service concocted and peddled a confection called the *Protocols of the Elders of Zion.*"

61

not be allowed to turn out into the world green young men with ideas on new constitutional reforms, as though these were comedies or tragedies, or who concern themselves with political questions, of which even their fathers had no understanding.

A wrong acquaintance of politics among a mass of people is the source of Utopian ideas and makes them into bad subjects. This you can see for yourselves from the educational system of the Gentiles. We had to introduce all these principles into their educational system, in order that we might as successfully destroy their social structure as we have done. When we are in power we will remove from educational programmes all subjects which might upset the brains of youth and will make obedient children out of them, who will love their ruler and recognise in his person the main pillar of peace and of public welfare.

Instead of classics and the study of ancient history, which contains more bad examples than good, we will introduce the study of the problems of the future. We will erase from the memory of man, the bygone ages, which may be unpleasant to us, leaving only such facts as would show the errors of the Gentile governments in marked colours. Subjects dealing with questions of practical life, social organisation and with the dealings of one man with another, as also lectures against bad selfish examples—which are infectious and cause evil, and all other similar questions of an instinctive character will be in the forefront of our educational programme. These programmes will be specially drawn up for the different classes and castes, the education of which will be kept strictly apart.

It is most important to lay stress on this particular system. Each class or caste will have to be educated

The mind is all powerful. Cherish it and nurture your mind, especially in these final days. "You will keep him in perfect peace, whose MIND is stayed on you..."

- Isaiah 26:3

In spite of all the refuting by various governments of the *Protocols*, the use and publication of the *Protocols* has continued to expand worldwide!

Joseph Goebbels, Adolph Hitler's Minister of Propaganda, readily accepted the *Protocols*. He quickly saw these *Protocols* as a lie to create an attitude among the German people of paranoia; which eventually enabled him to be the mass murderer that he became.

separately, according to its particular position and work. A chance genius always has known and always will know how to penetrate into a higher caste but, for the sake of this quite exceptional occurrence, it is not expedient to mix the education of the different castes and to admit such men into higher ranks, in order that they may only occupy the places of those who are born to fill them. You know for yourselves how fatal it was for the Gentiles when they gave way to the absolutely idiotic idea of making no difference between the social classes.

In God's eyes, there are no classes of society. We are all ONE with Him.

In order that the sovereign should gain a firm place in the hearts of his subjects it is necessary that, during his reign, the nation should be taught, both in schools as well as in public places, the importance of his activity and the benevolence of his enterprise.

We will abolish every kind of private education. On holidays, students and their parents will have the right to attend meetings in their colleges as though these were clubs. At these meetings professors will deliver speeches, purporting to be free lectures, on questions of men's dealings with one another, on laws and on misunderstandings which are generally the outcome of a false conception of men's social position, and finally they will give lessons on new philosophical theories, which have not yet been revealed to the world. These theories we will make into doctrines of faith, using them as a stepping-stone to our Faith.

Abolishing private education is serious. Have you ever known of a government program that is better run than a privately-funded program?

When I have finished taking you through the whole programme and when we shall have finished discussing all our plans for the present and for the future, I will read to you the plan of that new philosophical theory. We know from the experience of many centuries, that men live and are guided by ideas and that people are inspired by

Anti-Semitism was the "order of the day" under Adolph Hitler.

Alfred Rosenberg, chief ideologist for the Nazis, carried a copy of the *Protocols* to Munich in 1918. He came in contact with Rudolph Hess, the future deputy of the Fuhrer; and Hess immediately supported the document.

these ideas only by means of education, which can be given with the same result to men of all ages, but of course by various means. By systematical education we shall take charge of whatever may remain of that independence of thought, of which we have been making full use for our own ends for some time past. We have already established the system of subduing men's minds by the so-called system of demonstrative education (teaching by sight), which is supposed to make the Gentiles incapable of thinking independently and so they will, like obedient animals, await the demonstration of an idea before they have grasped it. One of our best agents in France is Bouroy: he has already introduced the new system of demonstrative education.

* * * * *

The profession of the law makes people grow cold, cruel, and obstinate and also deprives them of all principles and compels them to take a view of life which is not human, but purely legal. They have become used to look on circumstances purely from the point of view of what is to be gained from defence and not from that of the effect which such a defence might have on the public welfare.

A legal practitioner never refuses to defend any case. He will try to obtain an acquittal at all costs by clinging on to small tricky points in jurisprudence and by these means he will demoralise the court.

Therefore we will limit the sphere of action of this profession and will place lawyers on a footing with executive officials. Barristers, as well as judges, will have no right to interview their clients and will receive their briefs only when they are assigned to them by the law court and they will study these solely from reports and documents, and

You, my Friend, were made in the likeness and in the image of God!

Protocol # 17 - ABUSE OF AUTHORITY

Lawyers normally represent the best interests of the individual. Kiss that freedom good-bye via Protocols.

Infamous Nazi leader Heinrich Himmler, while resting from a sickness in 1919, was also influenced by the anti-Semitic work based on the *Protocols* in which Jews, Freemasons, and Democrats were reviled as the agents of world revolution. Himmler wrote in his diary about the *Protocols*: "A book that explains everything and tells us whom we must fight against next time."

will defend their clients after they have been examined in court by the prosecution, basing the defence of their clients on the result of this examination. Their fee will be fixed, regardless of the fact whether the defence has been successful or not. They will become simple reporters on behalf of justice, counterbalancing the prosecutor, who will be a reporter on behalf of the prosecution.

Thus legal procedure will be considerably shortened. By this means we shall also attain an honest impartial defence, which will be conducted not by material interests, but by the personal conviction of the lawyer. This will also have the advantage of putting an end to any bribery or corruption, which can at present take place in the law courts of some countries.

We have taken great care to discredit the clergy of the Gentiles in the eyes of the people, and thus have succeeded in injuring their mission, which could have been very much in our way. The influence of the clergy on the people is diminishing daily.

To-day freedom of religion prevails everywhere, and the time is only a few years off when Christianity will fall to pieces altogether. It will be still easier for us to deal with the other religions, but it is too early to discuss this point.

We will confine the clergy and their teachings to such a small part in life and their influence will be made so uncongenial to the populace that their teachings will have the opposite effect to what it used to have.

When the time comes for us to completely destroy the Papal Court, an unknown hand, pointing towards the Vatican, will give the signal for the assault. When the people in their rage throw themselves on to the Vatican, we shall appear as its protectors in order to stop bloodshed.

The Bible says "The steps of a righteous man are ordered of the Lord!" Are yours?

Heaven and earth shall pass away, but my Word will STAND!

This is a direct attack on the Vatican, the Pope, and all Catholics in the world.

The *Protocols* was one basis from which the Nazis gained an undeniable, powerful sense that total world domination was possible. That successful enterprise rests upon the willingness to deal mercilessly with adversaries and the ability to obtain the unconditional loyalty of followers.

By this act we will penetrate to the very heart of this Court and then no power on earth will expel us from it, until we have destroyed the Papal might. The King of Israel will become the true Pope of the universe, the Patriarch of the International Church.

But until we have accomplished the re-education of youth by means of new temporary religions, and subsequently by means of our own, we will not openly attack the existing Churches, but will fight them by means of criticism, which already has and will continue to spread dissensions among them.

Generally speaking, our press will denounce governments, religious and other Gentile institutions by means of all kinds of unscrupulous articles, in order to discredit them to such an extent as our wise nation only is capable of doing.

Our government will resemble the Hindu god Vishnu. Each of our hundred hands will hold one spring of the social machinery of State.

We shall know everything, without the aid of official police, which we have so corrupted for the Gentiles that it only prevents the government from seeing real facts. Our programme will induce a third part of the populace to watch the remainder from a pure sense of duty and from the principle of voluntary government service.

Then it will not be considered dishonourable to be a spy, on the contrary it will be regarded as praiseworthy. On the other hand, the bearers of false reports will be severely punished, in order to prevent abuse being made of the privilege of report.

Our agents will be selected both from among the upper and the lower classes; they will be taken from among administrators, editors, printers, booksellers, clerks, work-

The Jewish people are a peace-loving people. Even though there are stark differences between Catholics and Jews, no Jew would want to kill the Pope!

Protocols stoops so low as to have individuals spying on each other, much like the old "Communist block" system in the 1900's!

The *Protocols* also became a part of the Nazi propaganda effort to justify persecution of the Jews. In The Holocaust: The Destruction of European Jewry 1933-1945, Nora Levin states that "Hitler used the *Protocols* as a manual in his war to exterminate the Jews."

men, coachmen, footmen, etc. This force of police will have no independent power of action, and will not have the right to take any measures of their own accord, and therefore the duty of this powerless police will consist solely in acting as witnesses and in issuing reports. The verification of their reports and actual arrests will depend on a group of responsible police inspectors; actual arrests will be made by "gendarmes" and city police. In case of failure to report any misdemeanour, concerning political matters, the person who should have reported the same will be punished for wilful concealment of crime, if it can be proved that he is guilty of such concealment. In like manner our brothers have to do now, namely, on their own initiative to report to the proper authority all apostates and all proceedings that might be contrary to our law. So in our Universal Government it will be the duty of all our subjects to serve their sovereign by taking the above-mentioned action.

An organisation such as this will root out all abuse of power and various kinds of bribery and corruption—in fact it will destroy all ideas with which we have contaminated the life of the Gentiles, by means of our theories on superhuman rights.

How could we achieve our aim of creating disorder in the administrative institutions of the Gentiles if not by some such means as this?

Among the most important means for corrupting their institutions is the use of such agents as are in a position, through their own destructive activity, to contaminate others by revealing and developing their own corrupt tendencies, such as abuse of power and a free use of bribery.

* * * * *

A One World Government will show outright hatred towards the Jews!

* Protocols say that bribery is okay for the end objectives, much like Shariah Law NOW!

Mein Kampf is part autobiography and part political ideology by Adolph Hitler. Volume 1 was published in 1925, while Volume 2 was published in 1926. This book set the framework for the Third Reich; and eventually, World War Two.

This war resulted in the murder of over six million Jews!

When the time comes for us to take special police measures by putting the present Russian system of "Okhrana" in force (the most dangerous poison for the prestige of the state) we will stir up mock disorders among the populace, or induce it to show protracted discontent, and this with the aid of good orators. These orators will find plenty of sympathisers, thus giving us an excuse for searching people's houses and placing them under special restrictions by making use of our servants among the police of the Gentiles.

As most conspirators are actuated by their love for such art and for that of chattering, we will not touch them until we see that they are about to take action, and we will confine ourselves to introducing among them a, so to speak, reporting element. We must remember that a power loses prestige every time that it discovers a public conspiracy against itself. In such a revelation lies the presumption of weakness and, what is still more dangerous, the admission of its own mistakes. It must be known that we have destroyed the prestige of reigning Gentiles by means of a number of private assassinations, accomplished by our agents, the blind sheep of our flock, who can easily be induced to commit a crime, so long as such a crime is of a political character.

We will force rulers to admit their own weakness by openly introducing special police measures, "Okhrana," and thus we shall shake the prestige of their own power.

Our sovereign will be protected by means of most secret guards, as we will never allow anyone to think that there might exist such a conspiracy against our ruler that he could not personally destroy and from which he is obliged to hide himself. If we were to allow the existence of such an idea to prevail, as it prevails among the Gentiles,

Protocol # 18 - ARREST OF OPPONENTS

Private assassinations are against Scripture and the Ten Commandments.

In Mein Kampf, Hitler used the main thesis of "The Jewish Peril," which speaks of an alleged Jewish conspiracy to gain world leadership. The narrative describes the process by which he became increasingly anti-Semitic and militaristic, especially during his years in Vienna. This book proclaimed his hatred for two main problems in the world: Communism and Judaism.

we should thereby sign the death warrant of our sovereign or, if not of himself, then of his dynasty.

By a strict observance of appearances our ruler will use his power only for the benefit of the nation, but never for his own good or for that of the dynasty.

By strictly adhering to such a decorum, his power will be honoured and protected by his subjects themselves. They will worship the power of the sovereign, knowing that to this power is tied the welfare of the state, because from it will depend public order.

To guard the King openly is equivalent to an admission of the weakness of his power.

Our ruler will always be amidst his people and will appear to be surrounded by an inquisitive crowd of men and women, apparently always by chance occupying the rows nearest to him and thus holding back the mob with a view to keeping order merely for order's sake. This example will teach others to exercise self-control. In case of a petitioner amongst the people trying to submit a demand and pushing through the mob, the people in the first rows will take his petition and will remit it to the ruler in the presence of the petitioner, in order that everyone should know that all petitions reach the sovereign and that he himself controls all affairs. In order to exist, the prestige of power must occupy such a position, that the people can say among themselves: " If only the King knew about it " or " When the King knows about it."

The mysticism, which surrounds the person of the sovereign, vanishes as soon as a guard of police is seen to be placed round him. When such a guard is employed, any assassin has only to exercise a certain amount of audacity, in order to imagine himself stronger than the guard; he thus realises his strength and so only has to

Hitler refers to the *Protocols* in Mein Kampf: "...To what extent the whole existence of this people is based on a continuous lie is shown incomparably by the *Protocols* of the Wise Men of Zion, so infinitely hated by the Jews. They are based on a forgery; the Frankfurter Zeitung moans and screams once every week: the best proof that they are authentic. (...) the important thing is that with positively terrifying certainty they reveal the nature and activity of the Jewish people and expose their inner contexts as well as their ultimate final aims."

watch for the moment, when he can make an assault on the said power.

We do not preach this doctrine to the Gentiles, and you can see for yourselves the results, which the employment of open guards has had for them.

Our government will arrest such people as they may more or less rightfully suspect of political crimes. It is not desirable for fear of misjudging a man to give an opportunity of escape to such suspects.

We will, indeed, show no mercy to such criminals. In certain exceptional cases it may be possible to consider attenuating circumstances, when dealing with ordinary criminal offences; but there can be no excuse for a political crime, that is to say, no excuse for men to become involved in politics, which none, except the ruler, should understand. And, indeed, not all rulers are capable of understanding true politics.

* * * * *

We will prohibit individuals from becoming involved in politics, but, on the other hand, we will encourage every kind of report or petition submitting suggestions for the approval of the government which deal with the improvement of social and national life. Thus, by these means, the mistakes of our Government and the ideals of our subjects will become known to us. We will answer these suggestions by accepting them or, if they are unsatisfactory, by producing a sound argument to prove that they are impossible of realisation and based on a short-sighted conception of affairs.

Sedition is no more than the barking of a dog at an elephant. In a government that is well organised from a social point of view, but not from a point of view of its police, the dog barks at the elephant without realising

Protocol #19 - RULERS AND PEOPLE.

Protocols say that NO ONE can become involved in politics.

I urge you to exercise all your political freedoms to not only vote, but be pro-active in these end times!

In November, 1939, Hitler called for the distribution of the *Protocols* abroad in order to show that the real instigators of the war were the Jews and the Freemasons. It served to justify the preemptive strike against an invisible Jewish conspiracy and later, those thought to be its Bolshevik agents.

The *Protocols* fanned the flames of paranoia, transforming fear into hate. It is possible to map the progression from the Russian Imperial Palace to Auschwitz; or, from the Russian czars to Adolph Hitler.

his strength. The elephant has only to show its strength by one good example for the dogs to stop barking and to start wagging their tails as soon as they see the elephant.

In order to deprive the political criminal of his crown of valour, we will place him in the ranks of other criminals on an equal footing with thieves, murderers, and other kinds of repulsive·malefactors. Then public opinion will mentally regard political crimes in the same light as ordinary crimes and will place the same common stigma on both.

We have done our best to prevent the Gentiles from adopting this particular method of dealing with political crimes. In order to attain this end, we have made use of the press, public speaking, and cleverly thought-out history school-books, and inspired the idea of a political murderer being a martyr, because he died for the idea of human welfare. Such an advertisement has multiplied the number of liberals and has swollen the ranks of our agents by thousands of Gentiles.

* * * * *

To-day I will deal with our financial programme, which I have left for the end of my report, as being the most difficult question and forming the final clause in our plans. Before discussing this point, I will remind you of that which I have touched upon before, namely, that our whole policy is dependent on a question of figures.

When we get into power our autocratic government will, for the sake of self-interest, avoid imposing heavy taxation on the populace, and will always bear in mind that part which it has to play, namely, the part of father protector.

But, as the organisation of the Government will absorb vast sums of money, it is all the more necessary to raise

Protocol # 20 -
FINANCIAL PROGRAMS

"Father protector" really means "Big Brother is watching!"

Thomas Jefferson once said: "A government big enough to give you everything you want, is big enough to take away everything you have."

Think about it!

I'm sure that Adolph Hitler was thinking of the *Protocols* when he desperately urged: "Above all, I demand of the nation's leaders and followers scrupulous adherence to the race laws and to ruthless resistance against the world poisoners of all peoples, international Jewry."

In 1933, Hitler and Himmler made the *Protocols* required reading for Hitler's Youth Movement.

Until the very end, Nazi propagandist Joseph Goebbels kept a diary. In the ruins of defeated Nazi Germany, American intelligence found the private diary of the infamous Goebbels.

the required means for maintaining it. Therefore we must exercise great care in working out this question and see that the burden of taxation is fairly distributed.

Through a legalised fiction, our sovereign will be the owner of all property in the state (this is easily put into practice). He will be able to raise such sums of money as may be necessary to regulate the circulation of currency in the country.

Hence the best means to meet government expenses will be by a progressive taxation of property. Thus, taxation will be paid without oppressing or ruining the people and the amount at which it will be assessed will depend on the value of each individual property.

It must be understood by the rich that it is their duty to hand over part of their surplus wealth to the government, because the government guarantees them safe possession of the remainder of their property and gives them the right to earn money by honest means. I say honest, because the control of property will preclude robbery on legal grounds.

This social reform must be in the forefront of our programme, as it is the principal guarantee of peace and will brook no delay.

Taxation of the poor is the origin of all revolution and always greatly conducive to injury to the Government, as the latter, while trying to raise money from the poor, loses its chance of obtaining it from the rich.

Taxation of capital will diminish the increase of wealth in private hands, into which we have up till now purposely allowed it to accumulate, in order to act as a counterpoise to the Government of the Gentiles and their finances.

Progressive taxation assessed according to the fortune of the individual will produce a much larger revenue than

When a One World Government controls every dollar, greed takes over—and the individual pays the price!

In Volume 13, he writes: "I have devoted exhaustive study to the *Protocols of Zion*. In the past the objection was always made that they were not suited to present-day propaganda. In reading them now I find that we can use them very well. The *Protocols of Zion* are as modern today as they were when published the first time! At noon I mentioned this to the Fuhrer. He believed the *Protocols* to be absolutely genuine!"

the present system of taxing everybody at an equal rate. This system is at the present time (1901) most essential for us, it creates discontent among the Gentiles.*

Our sovereign's power will rest mainly on the fact that he will be a guarantee for the balance of power and for the perpetual peace of the world and, in order to obtain such a peace, capitals will have to surrender some of their wealth so as to safeguard the government in its action.

Protocols advise that the rich should be overly taxed.

Government expenditure must be paid for by those who can best afford to do so and from whom money can be raised.

Such a measure will stop hatred on the part of the poorer classes for the rich, in whom they will recognise the necessary financial supporters of the government and will see the upholders of peace and public welfare; for the poorer classes will understand that the rich provide the means for supplying them with social benefits.

In order that the intelligent classes, that is to say, the taxpayers, should not complain excessively about the new system of taxation, we will furnish them with detailed accounts, in which will be set forth the manner in which their money is being spent, excepting of course such portion of it as is spent on the private needs of the sovereign and on the requirements of the administration.

The sovereign will have no personal property, as everything in the state will belong to him, for if the sovereign were allowed to own private property it would appear as though all property in the state did not belong to him.

The relations of the sovereign—except his heir, who

* Note that this lecture was delivered in 1901.

During World War Two, there was a lot of contact between the Nazis and many Arab leaders. The most notorious was the Grand Mufti of Jerusalem, Hadj Amin Al-Husseini, who collaborated directly with Hitler. After World War Two, Hitler's ruthless extermination of the Jewish people, some six million, was somehow "justified" in some Arab countries.

will also be kept at government expense—will have to serve as government officials or else work in order to retain the right of holding property, the privilege of being of royal blood would not entitle them to live at the expense of the state.

There will be a progressive stamp duty on all sales and purchases as well as death duties. Any transaction without the required stamp will be considered illegal, and the former owner will be obliged to pay to the government a percentage on the duty from the date of the sale.

All transfer vouchers must be delivered weekly to the local surveyors of taxes, together with a statement of the name and surname of both the new and previous owner, as well as the permanent addresses of both.

Such a procedure will be necessary for transactions in excess of a certain amount, that is to say, in excess of the amount equal to the average daily expenditure. The sale of prime necessities will only have to be stamped with an ordinary fixed duty stamp.

Just count by how many times the amount of such taxation will surpass the income of the governments of the Gentiles.

The state will have to keep in reserve a certain amount of capital and, in case the income from taxation were to exceed this specified sum, such superfluous income will have to be put back into circulation. These surplus sums will be expended on the organisation of various kinds of public works.

The directorate of such works will be under a government department, and thus the interests of the working classes will be closely connected with those of the government and with their sovereign. A portion of this

The Protocols mentioned the anti-Christ. Could this "required stamp" signify the "Mark of the Beast?"

As the Jewish people began to immigrate to Palestine, many Arabs opposed this; and still do, obviously! The *Protocols* was translated into Arabic and became an instant best-seller in the Arab world. The myth of a Jewish worldwide conspiracy simply played into the hands of Islamists, globally.

Today's Jewish-Arab conflict is heightened by the acceptance of the Arab world of the *Protocols* as the absolute truth.

Regardless of what the "Sovereign" dictates, we still hold true to what the Bible says in I Timothy 5:17: "A laborer is worthy of his wages."

surplus money will also be allotted to premiums for inventions and productions.

It is most essential not to allow currency to lie inactive in the state bank, beyond such a specified sum as may be intended for some special purpose. For currency exists for circulation and any congestion of money always has a fatal effect on the course of state affairs, since money acts as a lubricant in the state mechanism and, if the lubricant becomes clogged, the working of the machine is thereby stopped.

The fact that bonds have been substituted for a large part of the currency has now created a congestion such as just described. The consequences of this fact are becoming sufficiently obvious.

We will also institute an auditing department, so as to enable the sovereign at any time to receive a full account of the expenditure of the government and its revenue. All reports will be kept strictly up to date, except those of the current and preceding months.

The only person who could not be interested in robbing the state bank will be its owner, namely, the Sovereign. For this reason his control will stop all possibility of leakage or unnecessary expenditure. Receptions for the sake of etiquette, which waste the valuable time of the Sovereign, will be abolished in order that he may have more opportunity to attend to affairs of state. Under our government the Sovereign will not be surrounded by courtiers, who usually dance attendance on the monarch for the sake of pomp and are only interested in their own affairs, putting aside as they do the welfare of the state.

All economic crises, which we have so skillfully arranged in the Gentile countries, we carried out by means of withdrawing currency from circulation. Large fortunes

Hamas has a political platform called "The Movement of Islamic Resistance" (formed in 1988), which continues to cause quite an anti-Semitic uproar. It borrows the ideas from *Protocols* almost word-for-word. It reads:

"The Jews have taken over the world media and financial centers. By fomenting revolutions, wars and such movements as the Free Masons, Communism, Capitalism and Zionism, Rotary, Lions, B'nai B'rith, etc., they are subverting human society as a whole in order to bring about its destruction, propagate their own viciousness and corruption, and take over the world via such of their pet institutions as the League of Nations, the United Nations and the Security Council. Their schemes are detailed in the *Protocols of the Elders of Zion*."

are congested, money being withdrawn from the government, which in its turn is obliged to appeal to the owners of such fortunes, in order to raise loans. These loans have put heavy burdens on the governments, compelling them to pay interest on the borrowed money, and thus tying their hands.

Concentration of production into the hands of capitalism has sucked all the productive power of the people dry, and with it also the wealth of the state.

Currency at the present time cannot satisfy the requirements of the working classes, as there is not enough to go all round.

The issue of currency must correspond to the growth of the population, and children have to be reckoned as consumers of currency from the first day of their birth. Occasional revision of currency is a vital question for the whole world.

I think that you know that gold currency has been the destruction of all states which have adopted it, because it could not satisfy the requirements of the population, all the more so because we have done our best to cause it to be congested and to be withdrawn from circulation.

Our government will have a currency based on the value of the working power of the country, and it will be of paper or even of wood.

We will issue currency sufficient for each subject, adding to this amount on the birth of every child, and diminishing it with the death of each person.

Government accounts will be kept by separate local governments and by county offices.

In order that delays should not occur in paying government expenses, the Sovereign himself will issue orders as to the term of payment of such sums, thus the

These "financial programs" set down by the Protocols continue to masquerade this unbelievable fraud.

Right now, one of the world's most aggressive terrorist organizations, Hamas, has its roots in the *Protocols*!

Article 32 of the Hamas Charter, adopted in 1988, specifies that the Zionists have laid out in detail "their scheme" in the *Protocols* of the Elders of Zion. Article 22 says the Zionist "scheming" had been going on "for a long time," specifically to accumulate "a huge and influential material wealth," which then "permitted them to take over control of the world media such as news agencies, the press, publication houses, broadcasting and the like."

In addition, according to the Charter, Zionists "established the League of Nations in order to rule the world." World War 2 was planned by the Zionists and when the combat ended, "they inspired the establishment of the United Nations and the Security Council...in order to rule the world by their intermediary."

favouritism which is sometimes shown by ministries of finance to certain departments will be terminated.

The revenue and expenditure accounts will be kept together, in order that they may always be compared with one another.

The plans which we will make for the reform of the financial institutions of the Gentiles will be introduced in such a manner as will never be noticed by them. We will point out the necessity of reforms, as being due to the disorderly state which Gentile finances have reached. We will show that the first reason for this bad state of finance lies in the fact that they start their financial year by making a rough estimate for the budget, the amount of which increases from year to year, and for the following reason: the annual budget is with great difficulty made to last till the end of the half year; then a revised budget is introduced, the money of which is generally expended in three months; after that a supplementary budget is voted; at the end of the year accounts are settled by a liquidation budget. The budget for the year is based on the total expenditure of the preceding year; therefore each year there is a deviation of about 50 per cent. from the nominal sum and the annual budget at the end of 10 years is increased threefold. Thanks to such a procedure, which was tolerated by the careless Gentile governments, their reserves have been drained. Then, when the period of loans arose, it emptied their state banks and brought them to the verge of bankruptcy.

You will readily understand, that such a management of financial affairs, which we induced the Gentiles to pursue, cannot be adopted by our Government.

Each loan proves the weakness of the government and its failure to understand its own rights. Each loan, like

"The rich rules over the poor. And the borrower is servant to the lender."
- Proverbs 22:7.

Is your financial house in order for the last days?

Hamas refuses to recognize Israel as a nation. It refuses to reject terrorism. It even refuses to accept previous agreements reached by the Palestinian Liberation Organization (PLO). The Hamas Charter says in its preamble that it plans to bring about the "ELIMINATION" of Israel. According to the charter, no compromise is possible. Article 7 of the Charter cites its version of the presumed vision of Allah: Peace will not be attained "until all Muslims will fight the Jews (and kill them)."

Nine Arabic editions of the *Protocols* were printed between 1951 and 1971. Egypt's Nasser utilized the *Protocols* skeptically in Egypt during his dictatorship presidency which began in the 1950's.

the sword of Damocles, hangs over the heads of the rulers who, instead of raising certain sums direct from the nation by means of temporary taxation, come to our bankers cap in hand.

External loans are like leeches, which cannot be separated from the body of the government until they fall off of themselves or until the government manages to shake them off. But the governments of the Gentiles have no desire to shake off these leeches; on the contrary, they increase their number, and therefore their state is bound to die from self-inflicted loss of blood. For what is an external loan if not a leech? A loan is an issue of government paper which entails an obligation to pay interest amounting to a percentage of the total sum of the borrowed money. If a loan is at 5 per cent., then in 20 years the government will have unnecessarily paid out a sum equal to that of the loan, in order to cover the percentage. In 40 years it will have paid twice, and in 60 thrice that amount, but the loan will still remain as an unpaid debt.

From this calculation it is evident that such loans, under the existing system of taxation (1901), draw the last cents from the poor taxpayer in order to pay interests to foreign capitalists, from whom the state has borrowed the money, instead of collecting the necessary sum from the nation free of all interest in the shape of taxation.

As long as loans were internal, the Gentiles only transferred money from the pockets of the poor into those of the rich; but after we bribed the necessary people to substitute external loans for internal, all the wealth of the states rushed into our safes and all the Gentiles started paying us what amounted to nothing short of tribute.

Other Islamic nations such as Libya, Saudi Arabia, and Tunisia also publicized the *Protocols* as a tool in their ongoing struggles with Israel.

In 1968, in Beirut, the Islamic Institute published 300,000 copies of the *Protocols* in Italian, French, Spanish, and Arabic.

On October 16, 2003, speaking to a meeting of the Organization of the Islamic Conference in Malaysia, then-Malaysian Prime Minister Mahathir Mohamad told the assembly of 57 nations that Islam must combat the Jews who today, "rule the world by proxy." Prime Minister Mahathir Mohamad also blamed international Jewish currency dealers for the recession in Malaysia.

Through their carelessness in statesmanship, or owing to the corruption of their ministers, or their ignorance of finance, Gentile Sovereigns have put their countries in debt to our banks, so that they can never pay off these mortgages. You must understand to what pains we must have gone in order to bring about such a state of affairs.

In our government we will take great care that congestion of money shall not occur, and therefore we will not have state loans, except one of 1 per cent. exchequer bonds, in order that payment of percentage should not expose the country to be sucked by leeches.

The right of issuing bonds will be given exclusively to commercial companies. These will have no difficulty in paying the percentage out of their profits because they borrow money for commercial enterprises, but the government cannot make profits from borrowed money, because it borrows solely in order to spend what it has taken on loan.

Commercial shares will also be bought by the government, which will thus become a creditor instead of being a debtor and payer of tribute as it is at present. Such a measure will put an end to indolence and laziness, which were useful to us as long as the Gentiles were independent, but would be undesirable in our government.

The emptiness of the purely bestial brains of the Gentiles is sufficiently proved by the fact that, when they borrowed money from us at interest, they failed to understand that each sum so borrowed, together with the interest on the amount, would eventually have to come out of the resources of the country. It would have been simpler to have taken the money from their own people at once without having to pay interest. This proves our genius,

In November, 2002, several Arab television channels began broadcasting "Knight Without a Horse," which is based upon the *Protocols of Zion*.

There have also been at least two major television productions for the Arabs in their language, in reference to the *Protocols*.

One is a 41-part series that appeared on Egyptian state television in 2002. The other was a 21-part Syrian television production that aired in 2003 on the Lebanon-based satellite network Al-Manar. This production created theatrical demonstrations for mass audiences based on the idea that the *Protocols* is indeed the secret plan of the Jews to control the world.

and the fact that our people has been elected by God. We have so managed as to present the question of loans in such a light to the Gentiles that they even thought that they found a profit in them.

Our estimates, which we will produce when the time comes, and which will have been worked out with the experience of centuries and which we have been considering while the Gentiles have been governing, will differ from those made by the Gentiles in their extraordinary clearness, and will prove to the world how beneficial are our new plans. These plans will terminate such abuses as those by which we became masters of the Gentiles, and as cannot be allowed in our reign. We will so arrange the system of our budget that neither the ruler himself nor the most insignificant clerk will be in a position unobserved to extract the smallest portion of the money or use it for any other purpose than that to which it has been allotted in the first estimate.

Did you know that God had more to say about your money in the Bible—than anything else?

Without a definitely fixed plan it is impossible to rule successfully. Even knights and heroes perish when they take a road not knowing where it leads, and start on their journey without being properly provisioned.

The Sovereigns of the Gentiles, whom we helped to induce to forsake their duties in the government by means of representations and entertainments, pomp, and other diversions, were no more than screens to hide our intrigues.

The reports of their followers, who used to be sent to represent the Sovereign in his public duties, were made for them by our agents. On each occasion these reports used to please the short-sighted minds of the sovereigns, accompanied, as they were, by various schemes for future economy. " How could they economise by fresh taxation ?"

In 1984, some sections of the *Protocols* appeared in the Iranian Journal, Imam.

B'nai B'rith Magazine reports on the anti-Semitism of Iran: "As early as 1986, a new Iranian edition of the *Protocols* was established in Teheran and widely distributed in the country by the official 'Islamic Propagation Organization, International Relations Department.' Some eight years later, one of the wealthiest institutions in Iran, the Shrine of Imam Reza, financed the publication of another edition of the *Protocols*. To strengthen the impact of the work, significant parts of the publication were reprinted in a radical daily journal under the heading, 'The Smell of Blood, Zionist Schemes.'

Protocol # 21 - LOANS AND CREDIT

This sentence in the Protocols directly conflicts with the Bible. "The Lord will open to you His good treasure, the heavens, to give the rain to your land in its season, and to bless all the work of your hand. You shall lend to many nations, but you shall not borrow."

- Deuteronomy 28:12

they could have asked, but they did not ask, the readers of our reports.

You yourselves know to what a state of financial chaos they have come by their own negligence, they have ended in bankruptcy in spite of all the hard work of their subjects.

* * * * *

I will now add to what I told you at our last meeting and give you a detailed explanation of internal loans. But I will not discuss external loans any further, because they have filled our coffers with Gentile money, and also because our universal government will have no foreign neighbours from whom they could borrow money.

We made use of the corruption of administrators and of the negligence of Gentile Sovereigns in order to obtain twice and three times the amount of the money advanced by us to their governments, which in reality they did not need at all. Who could do the same with regard to us? Therefore I will only go into the question of internal loans.

When it announces the issue of such a loan, the government opens a subscription for its bonds. In order that these bonds might come within the reach of everybody they are issued down to very small amounts. The first subscribers are allowed to buy below par. On the following day their price is inflated in order to convey the idea that everybody is anxious to buy them.

In the course of a few days the safes of the exchequer are full with all the money which has been oversubscribed. (Why continue accepting money for an oversubscribed loan?) The subscription is evidently considerably in excess of the amount asked for, in this lies the whole effect—the public evidently trust the government!

But when the comedy is over there arises the fact of a very large debt. And, in order to pay the interest on

Ahmadinejad's adoption of the *Protocols'* thesis is a natural progression. But the Iranian leader has taken the hate spewed in the document to other levels. Parallel to the *Protocols'* theme, he has called the Holocaust a "myth," claiming at an Islamic summit in Mecca that "we cannot accept...the claim" that "Hitler killed millions of innocent Jews in furnaces."

this debt, the government has to have recourse to a fresh loan, which, in its turn, does not annul the state debt, but only adds to it. When the borrowing capacity of the government is exhausted, the interest on the loans must be paid by new taxations. These taxations are nothing but debts contracted in order to cover other debts.

Then comes a period of conversions of loans, but such conversions only diminish the amount of interest to be paid, and do not annul the debt. Moreover they can only be made with the consent of the creditors. When such conversions are announced the creditors are given the right to accept them or to have their money back, in case they do not wish to accept the conversions. If everybody were to reclaim his own money, the government would be caught by its own bait, and would not be in a condition to return all the money. Luckily the subjects of the Gentile governments do not understand much of finance and they have always preferred suffering a fall in the value of their securities and a reduction of interest to the risk of a new investment; thus they have often given their government an opportunity to get rid of a debt, which probably amounted to several millions.

The Gentiles would not dare to do such a thing with external loans, knowing very well that, in such a case, we would demand all our money.

By such action the government would openly admit its own bankruptcy, which would plainly show the people that their own interests have nothing in common with those of their government. I specially draw your attention to this fact as also to the following: at present all internal loans are consolidated by so-called temporary loans, that is to say, debts, the period for the payment of which is short. These debts consist of the money placed on deposit

6

On December 11-12, 2006, Ahmadinejad became the first government leader ever to host a Holocaust-denial conference, inviting more than 65 well-known Holocaust deniers to challenge an accepted universal truth. The conference was called, Conference to Review the Global Vision of the Holocaust. It was held at the Iran Foreign Ministry's Institute for Political and International Studies (which immediately prompted an angry repudiation of the Institute by Western scholarly and academic groups).

According to Iran's Foreign Minister, Manouchehr Mottaki, the aim of the conference was to "create an opportunity for thinkers who cannot express their views freely in Europe," presumably because of the criminalization of Holocaust denial in several Western European democracies.

Protocols say how the Jews are supposed to have all their financial policies all planned out! Impossible!

82

in state banks or saving banks. This money, being at the disposal of the government for a considerable length of time, is used for paying interest on external loans and, in lieu of the money, the government places an equal amount in its own securities into these banks. These state securities cover all deficits in the state safes of the Gentiles.

When our sovereign is enthroned over the whole world, all these tricky financial operations will vanish. We will destroy the market in public funds, because we will not allow our prestige to be shaken by the rise and fall of our stocks, the value of which will be established by law at par without any possibility of fluctuation in price. Rise gives cause to fall, and it is by rises that we started to discredit the public funds of the Gentiles.

For Stock Exchanges will be substituted enormous government organisations, the duty of which will consist in taxing commercial enterprises as the government may think fit. These institutions will be in a position to throw on to the market millions' worth of commercial shares, or to buy up the same, in one day. Thus all commercial enterprises will be dependent on us.

You can imagine what a power we will thus become.

Protocol # 22 - POWER OF GOLD

* * * * *

In all which I have told you up till now I have tried to give you a true picture of the mystery of the present events, as also of those of the past, which all flow into the river of Fate, and the result of which will be seen in the near future. I have shown you our secret plans by which we deal with the Gentiles as well as our financial policy. I have only to add a few more words.

In our hands is concentrated the greatest might of the present days, that is to say, gold. In the course of

Iran's orientations to the *Protocols* are not as well-defined as those in the Hamas Charter. In a six-page November 29, 2006, letter addressed to "Noble Americans" and published on the Iranian United Nations delegation's website, Iranian President Mahmoud Ahmadinejad borrowed the language of the *Protocols* to condemn U.S. President George W. Bush's Middle East policy.

That policy, Ahmadinejad wrote, was forced upon America by "the Zionists" who have "imposed" themselves "on a substantial portion of the banking, financial, cultural, and media sectors" of United States' society." Ahmadinejad's diatribe against presumed Jewish domination of banks and media mirrors the central feature of the *Protocols* and its propagandists.

two days we can draw any amount of it from our secret treasure rooms.

Is it still necessary for us to prove that our rule is the will of God? Is it possible that, with such vast riches, we shall not be able to prove that all the gold, which we have been accumulating for so many centuries, will not help in our true cause for good,—that is to say, for the restoration of order under our rule?

It may require a certain amount of violence, but this order will eventually be established. We will prove that we are the benefactors who have restored lost peace and freedom to the tortured world. We will give the world the opportunity of this peace and freedom, but certainly only under one condition—that is to say, that it should strictly adhere to our laws. Moreover we will make it clear to everyone that freedom does not consist in dissoluteness or in the right of doing whatever people please. Likewise that the position and power of a man does not give him the right to proclaim destructive principles such as freedom of religion, equality, or similar ideas. We will also make it clear that individual freedom does not convey the right to any man to become excited or to excite others by making ridiculous speeches to disorderly masses. We will teach the world, that true freedom consists only in the inviolability of a man's person and of his property, who honestly adheres to all the laws of social life. That a man's position will be dependent on the conception which he has of another man's rights and that his dignity prohibits fantastic ideas on the subject of self.

Our power will be glorious, because it will be mighty and will rule and guide, but by no means follow leaders of the populace or any kind of orators who shout senseless words which they call high principles, and which are in

F 2

God says that "Pride comes before the fall." Look at the arrogance shown here!

Pray for your rulers every day. "Pray without ceasing" is the command of God in 1 Thessalonians 5:17!

Ahmadinejad, on September 22, 2011, at the United Nations' General Assembly, accused the United States of using the September 11, 2001 attacks as a pretext to launch wars on Iraq and Afghanistan.

Ahmadinejad's extremist anti-Semitic views have caused great disdain and reproach from the United Nations Security Council. The 15-Member Council criticized the public statements made by the Iranian leader denying the Holocaust and threatening the existence of a United Nations member state. Still, Ahmadinejad continues to publically call the Holocaust a "myth."

"Set your house in order, for you shall die and not live." – Isaiah 38:1

Protocol # 23 – INSTILLING OBEDIENCE

"...I am coming quickly, and My reward is with Me, to give to every one according to his work." – Revelation 22:12

reality nothing else but utopian ideas. Our power will be the organiser of order in which lies peoples' happiness. The prestige of this power will bring to it mystic adoration, as well as subjection of all nations. A true power does not yield to any right even to that of God. None will dare to approach it with the object of depriving it even of a thread of its might.

In order that people should become accustomed to obedience they must be trained to modesty, therefore we will reduce the production of objects of luxury. By these means we will also impose morals, which are being corrupted by continual rivalry on the grounds of luxury. We will patronise " peasant industries " in order to injure private factories.

The necessities for such reforms also lies in the fact that large private factory-owners often instigate their workmen against the government, perhaps, even unconsciously.

The populace engaged in local industries does not know the meaning of being " out of work," and this makes it cling to the existing order, and induces it to support the government. Unemployment is the greatest danger for the government. For us it will have done its work as soon as, by its means, we shall have obtained power.

Drunkenness will also be prohibited as a crime against humanity, and will be punishable as such; for man becomes equal to a beast under the influence of alcohol.

Nations only submit blindly to a strong power, which is absolutely independent of them and in whose hand they can see a sword, acting as a weapon of defence against all social insurrections. Why should they want their Sovereign to possess the soul of an angel? They must see in him the personification of strength and might.

The Anti-Defamation League comments: "Slews of articles have appeared since 9-11 telling of the great Jewish conspiracy that underlies the attack on the World Trade Center. Holocaust deniers in the Arab world and elsewhere attribute the acceptance by the world of the 'myth' of the Holocaust to Jewish control of the international media. Even in America this idea is alive, as when some critics of the war in Iraq blamed it on Jewish neo-conservatives, thereby absorbing central themes of the *Protocols* – of mysterious, excessive Jewish power and of Jews working against the interests of their country to serve Jewish interests."

A ruler must arise who will supersede the existing governments, which have been living upon a crowd, whose demoralisation we ourselves have brought about among flames of anarchy. Such a ruler must commence by extinguishing these flames, which are incessantly springing up from all sides.

In order to obtain such a result, he must destroy all societies which may be the origin of these flames, even if he has to shed his own blood. He must form a well-organised army, which will anxiously fight the infection of any anarchy, which may poison the body of the government.

Our Sovereign will be chosen by God and appointed from above in order to destroy all ideas influenced by instinct and not by reason, by brutal principles and not by humanity. At present these ideas successfully prevail in their robberies and violence under the banner of right and freedom.

Such ideas have destroyed all social organisations, thus leading to the reign of the King of Israel.

But their part will be played as soon as the reign of our Sovereign commences. Then we must sweep them away, so that no dirt should lie in our Sovereign's path.

Then we shall be able to say to the nations: "Pray to God and bow down before him who bears the mark of the predestination of the world and whose star God himself guided, in order that none other but Himself should be able to set humanity free from all sin."

* * * * *

Now I will deal with the manner in which we will strengthen the dynasty of King David, in order that it may endure until the last day.

Our manner of securing the dynasty will consist chiefly of the same principles which have given to our wise men

Protocol # 28 - QUALITIES OF THE RULER

There is always a seemingly "double standard" by many individuals and nations when they talk about the Jewish people. This is very evident today in the Middle East. Even in the Palestinian State question before the United Nations, people tend to overlook the senseless killings and terroristic acts by many neighboring nations of Israel; instead, they point their fingers at Israel for defending its borders and its people from blistering, rocket attacks.

the management of the world's affairs, that is to say, the direction and education of the whole human race.

Several members of the seed of David will prepare Kings and their successors, who will be elected not by right of inheritance but by their own capabilities. These successors will be initiated in our secret political mysteries and plans of governing, taking great care that no one else should acquire them.

Such measures will be necessary in order that all should know that only those can rule who have been initiated in the mysteries of political art. Only such men will be taught how to apply our plans in practice by making use of the experience of many centuries. They will be initiated in the conclusions drawn from all observations of our political and economical system and in all social sciences. In a word, they will be told the true spirit of the laws that have been founded by nature herself in order to govern mankind.

Direct successors to the sovereign will be superseded in the event of their proving to be frivolous or soft-hearted during their education, or in case they show any other tendency likely to be detrimental to their power, and which may render them incapable of ruling and even to be dangerous to the prestige of the crown.

Only such men as are capable of governing firmly, although perhaps cruelly, will be entrusted with the reins of government by our Elders.

In case of illness or loss of energy, our Sovereign will be obliged to hand over the reigns of government to those of his family who have proved themselves more capable.

The King's immediate plans and, still more, his plans for the future will not even be known to those who will be

Anne Frank's diary on May 22, 1944, reveals more of the same: "Oh, it is sad, that once more, for the umpteenth time, the old truth is confirmed: 'what one Christian does is his own responsibility, what one Jew does is thrown back at all Jews.'"

called his nearest councillors. Only our Sovereign, and the Three who initiated him, will know the future.

In the person of the Sovereign, who will rule with an unshakable will and control himself as well as humanity, the people will recognise as it were fate itself and all its human paths. None will know the aims of the Sovereign when he issues his orders, therefore none will dare to obstruct his mysterious path.

Of course, the Sovereign must have a head capable of dealing with our plans. Therefore he will not ascend the throne before his brain-power has been ascertained by our wise men.

In order that all his subjects should love and venerate their Sovereign, he must often address them in public. Such measures will bring the two powers into harmony, namely, that of the populace and that of the ruler, which we have separated in the Gentile countries by holding the one in awe of the other.

We had to hold these two powers in awe one of another, in order that they, when once separated, should fall under our influence.

The King of Israel must not be under the influence of his own passions, especially that of sensuousness. He must not allow animal instincts to get the better of his brain. Sensuousness, more than any other passion, is certain to destroy all mental and foreseeing powers; it distracts men's thoughts towards the worst side of human nature.

The Column of the Universe in the person of the World Ruler, sprung from the Holy seed of David, has to forgo all personal passions for the benefit of his people.

Our Sovereign must be irreproachable.

Signed by the representatives of
Zion, of the 33rd degree.

Anti-Semitism is NOT a Jewish problem. It is a global problem. Not that all Jewish people are perfect. Not all Jewish people act like they are "God's chosen people." But the global microscope is placed upon them, more than any other people group--wanting to find flaws. Yes, anti-Semitism is still very much alive and well; and continues to grow!

EPILOGUE.

These minutes were stealthily removed from a large book of notes on lectures. My friend found them in the safes at the headquarter offices of the Society of Zion, which is at present stituated in France.

France compelled Turkey to grant various privileges to the schools and religious institutions of all denominations, which will be under the protectorate of the French diplomacy in Asia Minor. Of course, these do not include the Catholic schools and institutions which were expelled from France by the late governments. This fact merely proves that the diplomacy of the Dreyfus schools is only anxious to protect the interests of Zion, and is working for the colonisation of Asia Minor by French Jews. Zion always knew how to acquire influence for itself by means of what the Talmud calls its " working brutes," by which it refers to the Gentiles in general.

According to the records of secret Jewish Zionism, Solomon and other Jewish learned men already, in 929 B.C., thought out a scheme in theory for a peaceful conquest of the whole universe by Zion.

As history developed, this scheme was worked out in detail and completed by men, who were subsequently initiated in this question. These learned men decided by peaceful means to conquer the world for Zion with the slyness of the symbolic serpent, whose head was to represent the initiated into the plans of the Jewish administration, and the body of the serpent to represent the Jewish people—the administration was always kept secret, even from the Jewish nation itself. As this serpent penetrated into the hearts of the nations which it encountered, it got under and devoured all the non-Jewish power of these states. It is foretold that the snake has

In western civilizations, the *Protocols* and anti-Semitism are "no big deal" to the uninformed. However, to the informed, and to those who have political interests in the Middle East, the *Protocols* is something that must be dealt with every single day. Shariah Law is overtaking the entire globe--and the *Protocols*, I believe, helped to shape some of those updated Shariah goals! It is not just PRO-radical Muslim ideals, it is significantly anti-Semitic!

to finish its work, strictly adhering to the designed plan, until the course which it has to run is closed by the return of its head to Zion and until, by this means, the snake has completed its round of Europe and has encircled it—and until, by dint of enchaining Europe, it has encompassed the whole world. This it is to accomplish by using every endeavour to subdue the other countries by an economical conquest.

The return of the head of the serpent to Zion can only be accomplished after the power of all the Sovereigns of Europe has been laid low, that is to say, when by means of economic crises and wholesale destruction effected everywhere there shall have been brought about a spiritual demoralisation and a moral corruption, chiefly with the assistance of Jewish women masquerading as French, Italians, etc. These are the surest spreaders of licentiousness into the lives of the leading men at the heads of nations.

Women in the service of Zion act as a decoy for those who, thanks to them, are always in need of money, and therefore are always ready to barter their conscience for money. This money is in reality only lent by the Jews, for it quickly returns through the same women into the hands of bribing Jewry—but, through these transactions, slaves are bought to the cause of Zion.

It is natural for the success of such an undertaking that neither the public officials nor private individuals should suspect the part played by the women employed by Jewry. Therefore the directors of the cause of Zion formed, as it were, a religious caste—eager followers of the Mosaic law and of the statutes of the Talmud. All the world believed that the mask of the law of Moses is the real rule of life of the Jews. No one thought of investigating

The present and future of world communication is the Internet. The medium has become the message. *Protocols* still has an appeal, especially on the Internet. The Internet serves as the postmodern substitute, replacing the anti-Semitic flyers.

the effect of this rule of life, especially as all eyes were directed on the gold, which could be supplied by the caste and which gave this caste absolute freedom for its economical and political intrigues.

A sketch of the course of the symbolic serpent is shown as follows :—Its first stage in Europe was in 429 B.C. in Greece, where, in the time of Pericles, the serpent first started eating into the power of that country. The second stage was in Rome in the time of Augustus about 69 B.C. The third in Madrid in the time of Charles V. in 1552 A.D. The fourth in Paris about 1700, in the time of Louis XVI. The fifth in London from 1814 onwards (after the downfall of Napoleon). The sixth in Berlin in 1871 after the Franco-Prussian war. The seventh in St. Petersburg, over which is drawn the head of the serpent under the date of 1881.

All these states which the serpent traversed have had the foundations of their constitutions shaken, Germany, with its apparent power, forming no exception to the rule. In economic conditions England and Germany are spared, but only till the conquest of Russia is accomplished by the serpent, on which at present all its efforts are concentrated. The further course of the serpent is not shown on this map, but arrows indicate its next movement towards Moscow, Kieff, and Odessa.

It is now well known to us to what extent the latter cities form the centres of the militant Jewish race. Constantinople is shown as the last stage of the serpent's course* before it reaches Jerusalem.

Only a short distance still remains before the serpent will be able to complete its course by uniting its head to its tail.

---

* Note that this map was drawn years before the Revolution in Turkey.

Anti-Semitic arguments are still advanced by tiny Aryan sects and the paranoia associated with the likes of Lyndon LaRouche, the John Birch Society, and the Liberty Lobby. However the political mainstream in America does not subscribe today to the *Protocols*.

In order to enable the serpent to pass easily over its course, the following measures were taken by Zion with the purpose of recasting society and converting the labour classes. First of all the Jewish race was so organised that none should penetrate into it and thus disclose its secrets. God himself is supposed to have told the Jews that they were predestined to rule over the whole earth in the form of an indivisible Kingdom of Zion. They have been told that they are the only race which deserves to be called human, all the rest being intended to remain "working brutes" and slaves of the Jews, and that their object must be the conquest of the world and the erection of the throne of Zion over the universe. (*See* Sanh. 91, 21, 1051.)

The Jews were taught that they are Supermen, and that they must keep themselves apart from all other nations. These theories inspired the Jews with an idea of self-glorification, because they are by right the sons of God. (*See* Jihal 67, 1; Sanh. 58, 2.)

The secluded mode of living of the race of Zion is strictly adhered to by the system of the "Kaghal," which compels every Jew to help his kinsman independent of the assistance which he receives from their local administrations, which screen the government of Zion from the eyes of those of the Gentile states, which, in their turn, always eagerly defend the Jewish self-government, erroneously regarding them as a purely religious sect. The above-mentioned ideas, instilled into the Jews, have also considerably influenced their material life.

When we read such works as "Gopayon," 14, page 1; "Eben-Gaizar," 44, page 81; "XXXVI. Ebamot," 98; "XXV. Ketubat," 36; "XXXIV. Sanudrip," 746; "XXX. Kadushin," 68A—which were all written in order

Of course there are those who still hold on to their hatred of the "Christ-killers," as well as many conservatives and liberals who are unwilling to offend their more prejudiced allies. The *Protocols* belongs to all of them. It is THEIR story and "working through" the past, their past, is ultimately their responsibility!

to glorify the Jewish race, we see that they really treat all Gentiles as though they were beasts, created only to serve them. They think that peoples, properties and even their lives belong to the Jews and that God permits His chosen race to make what use they like of them.

According to their laws all their ill-treatment of the Gentiles is forgiven them on the day of their New Year, at which time also indulgence is given them to sin likewise in the coming year.

In order to excite the hatred of their people towards all Gentiles, the leaders of the Jews acted as "agents-provocateurs" in anti-Semitic risings by allowing the Gentiles to find out some of the secrets of the Talmud. Expressions of anti-Semitism were also very useful to the leading Jews, because they created compassion in the hearts of some Gentiles towards the people who were being apparently ill-treated, thus enlisting their sympathies on the side of Zion.

The anti-Semitism, which brought about persecutions of the lower orders among the Jews, helped their leaders to control and hold their kinsmen in subjection. This they could afford to do, because they always intervened at the right time and saved their fellow people. Note that the leaders of the Jews never suffered from anti-Semitic risings as regarded their personal belongings or their official position in their administration. This is not to be wondered at, as these heads themselves set the "Christian bloodhounds" against the humbler Jews and the bloodhounds managed to keep their herds in order for them, and thereby helped to establish the solidity of Zion.

The Jews, in their own opinion, have already attained the position of a super-government over the whole world, and are now throwing away their masks.

But in the end, YOU must be responsible for "your" story of how you react to the message within the Protocols; and, more importantly, how you react to anti-Semitism!

Of course, the main conquering power of Zion always lay in their gold; therefore they only had to work in order to give a value to this gold.

The high price of gold is chiefly accounted for by gold currency; its accumulation in the hands of Zion is accounted for by the Jews being able to profit and make use of any serious international crisis in order to monopolise gold. This is proved by the history of the Rothschild family, published in Paris in the " Libre Parole."

By means of these crises the might of Capitalism was established under the banner of Liberalism and protected by cleverly thought-out economical and social theories. By giving these theories a scientific appearance the Elders of Zion obtained extraordinary success.

The existence of the balloting system always affords Zion an opportunity of introducing, by means of bribery, such laws as may suit its purpose. The form of Gentile government most after the Jews' own heart is a Republic, because with such they can the more easily manage to buy a majority and the republican system gives their agents and army of anarchists unlimited freedom. For this reason the Jews are such supporters of Liberalism and the stupid Gentiles, who are befooled by them, ignore the already evident fact that, under a republic there is no more freedom than under an autocracy; on the contrary, there exists an oppression of the few by the mob, which is always instigated by the agents of Zion.

According to the will of Montefiore, Zion spares no money or means in order to attain these ends. In our days all governments throughout the world, consciously or unconsciously, are subject to the orders of that great super-government which is Zion, because all their bonds are in the possession of the latter and all countries are

The work of the *Protocols* continues to expand globally. For instance--

In the 1930's a Spanish edition appeared. In 1972 another edition was published and used to explain certain Vatican reforms by the Catholic Church.

indebted to the Jews to such an extent as never to be able to pay off their debts. All trade, commerce, as well as diplomacy, are in the hands of Zion. By means of its capital it enslaved all Gentile nations. By dint of intensified education on a material basis the Jews laid heavy chains on all the Gentiles, with which they have attached them to their super-government.

The end of national freedom is at hand, and therefore also individual liberty will come to an end, because true liberty cannot exist where the lever of money renders it possible for Zion to govern the mob and to reign over the more worthy and more reasonable portion of the community. . . . "Those that have ears to hear, let them hear."

* * * * *

It will soon be four years since "the Protocols of the Elders of Zion" have been in my possession. God alone knows how numerous have been the unsuccessful attempts which I have made in order to bring them to light or even to warn those who are in power and reveal to them the causes of the storm which hangs over apathetic Russia, who seems unfortunately to have lost all count of what is going on around her.

And only now, when I fear that it is too late, have I succeeded in publishing my work, in the hope that I may be able to warn those who still have ears to hear and eyes to see.

There is no room left for doubt. With all the might and terror of Satan, the reign of the triumphant King of Israel is approaching our unregenerate world; the King born of the blood of Zion—the Anti-Christ—is near to the throne of universal power.

Events in the world are rushing with stupendous rapidity; dissensions, wars, rumours, famines, epidemics,

In 1937, a new Italian edition came out.

In the 1930's, a new edition surfaced in Argentina.

In 1972, it was published in Egypt.

and earthquakes—what was but yesterday impossible, has to-day become an accomplished fact. Days rush past, as it were for the benefit of the chosen people. There is no time to minutely enter into the history of humanity from the point of view of the revealed "mysteries of iniquity," to historically prove the influence which the "elders of Israel" have had on the misfortunes of humanity, to foretell the already approaching certain future of mankind or to disclose the final act of the world's tragedy.

The Light of Christ alone and that of His Holy Universal Church can penetrate into the Satanic depths and reveal the extent of their wickedness.

In my heart I feel that the hour has struck for summoning the Eighth Ecumenical Council to which, oblivious of the quarrels which have parted them for so many centuries, will congregate the pastors and representatives of the whole of Christianity, to meet the advent of the Anti-Christ.

* * * * *

NOTE.

The Protocols are 24 in number. Readers who wish to do so can indicate them on their own copies from the following table, which gives the pages where the divisions occur, and the line where there is no division shown in the text :—

Protocol I. begins	on page 1.	Protocol XIII. begins	on page 45.
Protocol II.	on page 8.	Protocol XIV.	on page 48.
Protocol III.	on page 10.	Protocol XV.	on page 50, l. 11
Protocol IV.	on page 16.	Protocol XVI.	on page 60.
Protocol V.	on page 18.	Protocol XVII.	on page 63.
Protocol VI.	on page 22, line 17.	Protocol XVIII.	on page 67.
Protocol VII.	on page 24.	Protocol XIX.	on page 69.
Protocol VIII.	on page 25.	Protocol XX.	on page 70.
Protocol IX.	on page 26, line 32.	Protocol XXI.	on page 80.
Protocol X.	on page 30.	Protocol XXII.	on page 82.
Protocol XI.	on page 37, line 5.	Protocol XXIII.	on page 84, l. 8
Protocol XII.	on page 39.	Protocol XXIV.	on page 85.

Printed by the Judaic Publishing Company, Limited, 28 Milkwood Road, London, S.E.

In 1974, the *Protocols* new edition was published in Bombay, India, entitled "International Conspiracy Against Indians."

In 1977, three editions of the Protocols in English in the United States were published.

In 1978, a new edition in England.

"In Bolshevism there lies to-day the hope of humanity."

"The ideals of Bolshevism, at many points, are consonant with the finest ideals of Judaism."—*Jewish Chronicle*.

Popular Edition, 10/- net.

THE JEWS' WHO'S WHO.

The First Edition of this epoch-making work being exhausted, a popular edition is now in the Press, and will be issued shortly at the reduced price of 10/- net. THE JEWS' WHO'S WHO was designed and compiled long before the famous "Protocols" were heard of in England, in order to show to Britons how completely the Jewish power has undermined and secured control of all the financial and political life of the British Empire. The body of the work contains the names and histories of leading Jews who have been active in the work of disintegrating the British Empire and changing it into a Jewish Dominion. It gives a list of some of their activities and includes some of their more or less British connections, partners, and patrons. Incidentally it provides a concrete proof and illustration of the "Protocols of the Elders of Zion," and of the working out of their diabolical policy.

The Introductory part of the work possesses great historical importance, and traces the working of the Jew Plot through the centuries. It shows that the Talmud is the Jews' "Gospel," and not the Old Testament, and that the Jews' "religion" is Finance and Politics and hatred of the Christian world. It gives a concrete instance of the triumph of the Jew over the Empire in the critical case of South Africa, where the Jews plotted and organised the Jameson Raid, the Boer War, the Rebellion, and—by means of bribery and corruption, aided by these wars—gained complete ascendancy over all South African wealth, trade and politics.

"The information given is singularly accurate, and its collection must have involved an immense amount of research."—*Financial News*.

Orders received by The Secretary, THE BRITONS, 62 Oxford Street, W.1.

Price, 2/6.

ENGLAND UNDER THE HEEL OF THE JEW. (Roworth).

A TALE OF TWO BOOKS.

The two books in question are "The Jews and Modern Capitalism," by the Jewish Professor Sombart, which traces the steps by which the Jews "fathomed all the secrets that lay hid in money, and found out its magic powers. They became LORDS OF MONEY, and through it LORDS OF THE WORLD." The other book, a South African work, shows how they succeeded in becoming LORDS OF SOUTH AFRICA.

"This is a book that every patriot will do well to read and lay to heart."—*Kelso Chronicle*.

In 1987, a Japanese language edition appeared in Japan.
In 1988, the Hamas edition was distributed.
In 1990, a new edition appeared in Damascus, Syria.
In 1992, a new Catholic edition in Mexico.
In 1992, in Russia and in Turkey.
On-and-on--country-after country--
the *Protocols* continue to be re-released.

CONCLUSION

The bottom line is a continued anti-Semitism which basically faults the Jewish people with all the ills that have come against any society in any country. Anti-Semitics believe that the Jews are behind every bad thing that happens today! Period.

No matter how fake the *Protocols* is...no matter how fraudulent the *Protocols* has been judged in court!

Anti-Semitism offers an expedient worldview for all those who feel themselves threatened by the forces of modernity, who fear the future, and who seek comfort in strict religious and anti-democratic forms of authority.

Those people will always find a "scapegoat." For various reasons and under unique conditions, Jews have usually "fit the bill."

There are still those anti-Semites and their willing audiences who remain willing to spread and believe this fantasy of hate.

Unfortunately, the *Protocols* will not go away!

This is amongst the most vicious anti-Semitic works that has ever been published, and it continues to be a best-seller around the world.

Even though it is a fraud and a fake!

Blaming the Jewish people, using them as a "scapegoat," will not solve any problems. It will make the problem even worse.

Making progress towards a better world full of peace requires work, forgiveness and the love of God.

May the God of Abraham, Isaac, and Jacob bless you mightily for standing with Israel!

—Mike Evans